Add a Spiritual Dimension to Ordinary Church Meetings

Beyond the Agenda

JESSIE SCHUT

CRC Publications
Grand Rapids, Michigan

Acknowledgments

CRC Publications is grateful to Jessie Schut for writing this book. Jessie is associate editor of *Living Light News* in Edmonton, Alberta, and is a regional church education consultant for the Christian Reformed Church. She has written four pamphlets in the series *So You've Been Asked To . . . Teach Church School, . . . Give the Children's Message, . . . Recruit Volunteers, . . . Be a Friendship Teacher* (CRC Publications). *God's Gift of Work* (CRC Publications) is the latest in a series of eight short courses she has written for Friendship, a program for adults with mental impairments. Jessie has also authored *A Pile of Stones: Devotions for Kids* (CRC Publications).

Unless otherwise indicated, Scripture quotations in this publication are from the HOLY BIBLE, NEW INTERNATIONAL VERSION. © 1973, 1978, 1984 by the International Bible Society. Used by permission of Zondervan Bible Publishers.

Scripture quotations from the New Revised Standard Version Bible, © 1989 by the Division of Christian Education of the National Council of the Churches of Christ in the United States of America. Used by permission of Zondervan Publishing House

We welcome your comments. Call us at 1-800-333-8300 or email us at editors@crcpublications.org.

Library of Congress Cataloging-in-Publication Data
Schut, Jessie, 1948-
    Beyond the agenda: add a spiritual dimension to ordinary church meetings / Jessie Schut.
       p.   cm.
    Includes bibliographical references.
    ISBN 1-56212-443-9
    1. Church meetings—Prayer-books and devotions—English. 2. Small groups—Religious aspects—Christianity—Prayer-books and devotions—English. 3. Fellowship—Religious aspects—Christianity—Prayer-books and devotions—English. I. Title.
    BV652.15.S38   1999
    254'6—dc21   99-056752

10 9 8 7 6 5 4 3 2 1

Contents

Introduction

It's 8:01 Thursday evening, and the education committee of Hope Community Church is assembled in the church basement. John arrives just as Yolanda, the chairperson, finishes praying for blessings on the meeting. John mumbles apologies while members shuffle their chairs to make room for him.

Yolanda, a bit ruffled by the interruption, launches into the three items on the agenda: recruitment, budget, and dealing with a letter from a disgruntled volunteer. Susan, stifling a yawn, hopes it will be a short meeting this time. She loves teaching church school but finds running the education program a drag.

But the meeting quickly bogs down when Gerald and Mary Ruth disagree on whether bulletin announcements or letters would be a better strategy for enlisting teachers. Then Jacob proposes changes to the budget accounting procedures—again! "What is it with this guy and his emphasis on the bottom line?" Susan wonders. The complaint letter puts everyone on edge, and time passes while the committee defends the education program—to each other.

Finally, at 10:15 Yolanda ends the meeting with another prayer. Everyone eagerly heads out the door, thankful that it's over for another two weeks.

Variations of this scene occur in thousands of churches every week. Good or bad, working group meetings—whether they're called committees, teams, councils, sessions, task forces, or something else—are a fact of church life.

It's how churches run these days. Yet, one study shows that "fewer than 7 percent of church members are energized by attending a committee meeting. Most committee members attend out of duty and then wonder why their faith seems to be deadened by spending time in this ministry" (Dan Poffenberger, Judy Stack Nelson, and Patrick Keifert, *Working Together: Leading a Task-Oriented Small Group*).

"Is this really the best way to do things?" the Geralds and Susans of the church wonder. They want to do God's work in this world, but they're so busy *doing* church that they have little time to *be* the church. Can't there be something more?

A Better Way

Working groups successfully carry out the business of institutions like government, business, and industry. Since the church is also an institution, it's appropriate to have working groups doing the tasks of the church. But the church is more than an institution—it is also the body of Christ! Working groups in the church are more than a gathering of people who carry out a specific task; they are also a community of believers.

Too often working groups in the church have adopted their style of operation from the business world rather than from the models they find in the Bible. They may "baptize" their meetings with prayer and Scripture, but then it's back to business as they deal with lengthy agendas and delegation of necessary tasks.

But it doesn't have to be that way. Consider the first community of believers described in Acts 2:42-47. Pentecost Community Church ate together, worshiped together, and shared their possessions. They celebrated and prayed and studied the Word together; they supported and encouraged each other. They met together with glad and sincere hearts.

But the stories in Acts also show that they got a lot of church work done, much of it likely through small working groups. They distributed food to widows, took collections for poor churches, made decisions about sending out missionaries beyond Judea, determined policies about circumcision and food offered to idols, and found ways to use the gifts of the people to build up the body. They didn't seem to tire of being and doing church.

Imagine if Pentecost Community Church had been the site of an education committee meeting. In such a community, John's late arrival might have sparked concern and prayers for him; it might have given him the opportunity to explain that his life is chaotic with his wife in the hospital. Gerald and Mary Ruth might have listened more carefully to each other and reached a consensus instead of sparring over how to recruit new volunteers. Jacob's comments about the budget may have given others a chance to affirm his accounting gifts. And the letter from the disgruntled volunteer might have stimulated the committee to set up guidelines and make specific changes to improve the education program.

In both Hope Community Church and Pentecost Community Church, the work gets done. But in Pentecost Community Church, the committee members feel the relational bonds that are so distinctively the mark of the body of Christ. And knowing that they are part of a supportive and caring community, they are energized rather than sapped of energy by the work they've undertaken.

Beyond the Agenda

This book was written to help your working small group become more reflective of the body of Christ. Part One considers what it means to be a Christian small group and outlines principles for building community in small groups while furthering the mission of the church. Practical suggestions provide direction for working small group leaders.

Part Two provides devotions and activities that will encourage your group to become a community. By building the agenda into a framework of prayer, reflection, discussion, sharing, and worship, accomplishing specific tasks will become only one part of the reason why your group meets together regularly.

We recognize that your group has an agenda to follow and tasks to accomplish. We propose that these tasks will be done more joyfully, with a greater sense of purpose, and with more satisfying results if your working group is a community of caring people who support each other. And in the process, your group will move beyond the agenda to become a model of Christ's body here on earth.

Part One:
Direction for the Working Small Group

- What's in a Name?
- Building Community–and the Kingdom
- It's All About Love–and Seating Plans
- Down to the Nitty-Gritty–Doing It!

What's in a Name?

A s we noted in the Introduction, working groups in the church—regardless of what they are called—have a specific function. But does the name have more to say about the group than we might think?

Group or Small Group?

In *Understanding Human Communication*, Ronald Adler and George Rodman use the name *group* for "a small collection of people who interact with each other, usually face to face, over time in order to achieve goals." By this definition, the education committee at Hope Community Church is definitely a group. Its six members meet together twice a month to oversee and facilitate the congregation's education program.

Hope's education committee could also be categorized as a *small group*. Small group ministry has become a prominent movement within the church today. Some think it's just another fad that the church is going through; others believe it's the best way of doing church.

God created us to live in community, and Christians have always turned to each other for support and love. In fact, Scripture emphasizes that Christians need each other because alone, they are only one small part of the body of Christ. The head needs the heart, the hand needs the foot, and all the parts of the body work together to make a beautiful whole (1 Cor. 12:12-27).

Today's culture, however, encourages individualism and independence, and so the church has had to become more intentional in encouraging community. In a society that is growing more and more impersonal, small groups have sprung up to fill a need for community and belonging.

Members of large congregations know there is something very special about belonging to a small group of people who support and care for each other, who provide a safe community where they can grow and be loved. Even in small congregations, small groups can fulfil a vital function where people can be themselves, pray together, and encourage each other. (Other benefits of small groups are described in the box on p. 13.)

Various kinds of small groups exist in churches: groups that meet to study Scripture, groups that draw in seekers, support groups for those dealing with a common problem, disciple-making groups, and groups that are service oriented. This book was written to address the needs of this last type of group.

A Christian Small Group

Small group expert Roberta Hestenes gives this generally accepted definition of a Christian small group: "An intentional face-to-face encounter of no more than twelve people who meet on a regular basis with the purpose of growing in the knowledge and likeness of Jesus Christ" (Roberta Hestenes and Julie Gorman, *Building Christian Community Through Small Groups*). Unfortunately, members of the education committee of Hope Community Church—and many other working groups—just don't think of themselves as a small group that fits this definition. "Growing in the knowledge and likeness of Jesus Christ" isn't descriptive of their purpose. Instead, they think of themselves as a collection of people with a task to accomplish who often seem to struggle in their knowledge and likeness of Christ.

Hope's Gerald and Mary Ruth often have different approaches to problems, and Jacob's bottom-line approach to budgeting irritates most of the other members. Rarely do they feel like they're mirroring the body of Christ. In fact, they wonder sometimes if Jesus would recognize himself in them.

WHY SMALL GROUPS WORK

Small group expert David Stark and others have identified these seven biblically based sociological principles that explain why small groups work:

- **Synergism.** When individuals work together they are able to accomplish most tasks better and faster than individuals could acting alone.

- **Learning retention.** Group discussion allows people to ask questions, share doubts, explore applications, and hear additional insight.

- **Transformation.** In a small group environment, people will modify core parts of their lives, beliefs, behaviors, attitudes, norms, and responsibilities to a much greater extent and with a significantly higher success rate than they will alone.

- **Risk taking and experimentation.** People will take greater risks when they have a group of people who join them in the process than they will alone.

- **Problem solving and decision making.** A well-run small group can make better choices than individuals can by themselves. Problem solving and decision making in groups typically generates higher quality solutions and greater comprehension, ownership, and acceptance of the solutions.

- **Support and belonging.** All people have the need to belong, the need for a place they can call home. Small groups help people feel included and supported.

- **Accountability.** A small group in which the members hold one another accountable can help many people resist, to a greater degree, addictive, sinful, or unwanted behaviors and begin to embrace new ones.

—Poffenberger, Nelson, Keifert, *Working Together: Leading a Task-Oriented Small Group* (pp. 17-20). Used by permission.

So how can Hope Community's education committee—and your working group—become more like a small group that grows in the knowledge and likeness of Christ while accomplishing its tasks? First, your working group will become more of a unified community if you have a clear idea of your ministry, purpose, and vision; and second, your working group will feel more like a caring body of believers if the activities you do within your group build relationships. The next two chapters provide direction in these two areas.

Building Community—and the Kingdom

Y our working small group is not a stand-alone operation. It is part of a larger organization, the church. The church's purposes and ministry define the role that your working small group will be fulfilling. We'll look first at how this happens at Hope Community Church and then describe five key principles for building community in your small group while furthering God's kingdom.

Hope Community Church at Work

Hope Community Church was established more than forty years ago in a suburb of a large midwestern city. Hope owns its own church building and has earned a reputation as a well-established, strong congregation. It attracts an average of three hundred worshipers weekly. Hope Church has quite a number of working groups: an elders council, a diaconate, half a dozen committees, worship teams, and an administrative task force. Dozens of members have been recruited to help run the programs and ensure that all the ministries are able to function.

Most of this will sound familiar to people who are part of church culture. It's a common way to organize the business of doing church: small groups of workers are chosen from the larger body to ensure that the larger body can function effectively. But look beneath the surface of this picture, and you will find a complex infrastructure.

Hope Community Church is more than a forty-year-old institution that attracts three hundred worshipers on a given Sunday. And working groups are more than maintenance teams that keep an organization's wheels well-oiled so they run smoothly. Hope Church exists for a purpose: it is Christ's body on earth, founded by God to fulfill God's mission. All of the ministries at Hope—from church school and choir to worship services and the seniors circle—serve to promote and advance that purpose and mission. Seen from that perspective, the working groups within Hope Church become important avenues of service offered to further the kingdom of God.

Currently Hope Church is going through some changes. At its founding, most of the members were young families, but now the median age of the congregation is much older, and there are fewer children and teens. A new pastor is challenging the congregation to become more outreach oriented. Meetings have been held, and the church has adopted a new vision statement: "Hope Church will be a joyful community that draws in seekers and disciples believers to maturity." Other reports define the structure of the congregation, set out purposes and strategies, and outline policy statements. All of these documents have an impact on how committees and other task groups will set their goals and conduct their work.

Key Principles for Building Community

The description of Hope Community Church in operation illustrates five key principles that will help your small group become a working community. We'll look at each of these principles and provide some strategies for small group leaders.

1. **Members of a working group may have a diversity of gifts and abilities but should have a common passion for its work.**

The first key principle to building community within working groups is found in the composition of the group. When all members of a task group are enthusiastic about the same thing, they are well on the way to being a community.

Hope Church's education committee has six members representing a variety of backgrounds, occupations, and spiritual

16

gifts. However, they have one thing in common: all believe passionately that church education programs can make a huge impact on the spiritual growth of church members. When new members are recruited for vacant positions on the committee, this commitment to church education is a vital qualification for serving on the committee.

Unfortunately, working groups sometimes include people who are not passionately committed to the group's work. Some members may be serving out of a sense of duty or obligation. Somebody needs to do it, or it won't get done, is the rationale. Sometimes positions in certain working groups are "awarded" to those who have power, wealth, or status. Often people are asked to serve as a way of getting them involved in the work of the church, regardless of their gifts, passions, or spiritual maturity. When people serve in areas where their heart isn't leading them, they will be less committed to strengthening relationships with other members of the group.

When time and energy are spent in careful recruitment, it's more likely that the right people will become part of your working group. Perhaps your congregation has identified people's gifts using such tools as *Discover Your Gifts* (adult version by Alvin J. Vander Griend, CRC Publications, 1996; youth version by Ruth Vander Zee, CRC Publications, 1998). That's a good starting place, but effective recruiting involves more, as we've described in the box on page 18.

When you recruit effectively, your working group will be joined by people who are committed to your ministry and eager to carry out its tasks. And you'll find that it's much easier to build relationships within a group of people who share a passion and enthusiasm for your ministry.

2. The working group—a small part of a whole group—must work to further the goals and purposes of the larger group.

If Hope's working groups fail to take into account the congregation's new vision and stick to "business as usual," they may experience great frustration. If, on the other hand, they are committed to doing their part in fulfilling the congregation's new vision, they will be unified in a common mission that binds them together.

Consider the working group you lead. (The role of small group leader is described in the box on p. 19). Do group members have a

STEPS FOR RECRUITMENT

Following these steps for recruitment will help ensure that the right people are serving in a working group:

- Pray that God will provide the laborers for the work that needs to be done. The key qualification for these laborers is that they are people "full of faith and of the Holy Spirit" (Acts 6:5) rather than wealth or position.

- Consider people who have demonstrated in their lives and ministry that they desire to serve God. This is especially important in positions of leadership. Choose leaders who have served effectively in some ministry.

- Look for people who have the spiritual gifts needed to complete the tasks in your group. Spiritual gifts are given by God for the common good; it's how God designed the church. When all the members are using their gifts, the body—and working groups—will be strong and healthy.

- Inform prospective members about the realities and importance of the position. Discuss the job description, the time commitment expected, and the challenges facing your group.

- Care about the person. Express concern about the individual's availability, family and work situation, and spiritual health. Give the person time to consider and pray about the position.

- Provide adequate training for and orientation to the work required.

—Roberta Hestenes, *Turning Committees into Communities* (pp. 17-24)

Note: For more practical suggestions for effective recruiting, see Jessie Schut's *So You've Been Asked To . . . Recruit Volunteers* (CRC Publications, 1999). This pamphlet presents a positive perspective for the task of recruitment and provides a framework and practical strategies for recruitment.

clear understanding of your congregation's purpose and mission? Does each person support that purpose and mission whole-heartedly? (You may want to provide copies of the mission statement and allow time for members to discuss their reactions to it. This will set the stage for setting goals for your working group.)

TWO ESSENTIAL ROLES FOR SMALL GROUP LEADERS

Master of Change
Small group leaders need to see change as a friend, not an enemy. The master of change

- is committed to continuous improvement.

- empowers people to do what is right instead of "what we've always done."

- develops the skills required to make changes in ways that minimize counterproductive disruptions.

- motivates people to achieve.

- creates the support of the group and congregation leaders.

Person of Vision
A congregation's vision comes from all sorts of people in the congregation: the pastor, council members, small group leaders, and small group members. A person of vision

- has the necessary passion to get a difficult task accomplished.

- motivates the right people to action.

- creates new ministries.

- articulates the vision so others can understand it.

- builds consensus around the vision rather than around personality or other factors.

—Poffenberger, Nelson, Keifert, *Working Together: Leading a Task-Oriented Small Group* (p. 8). Used by permission.

Groups that see themselves as part of a bigger picture will have more enthusiasm and energy for their tasks, knowing that their work is accomplishing a higher purpose. These groups look beyond individual agendas and see that their task is to build the kingdom of God. Individual members of the group see themselves as fellow workers united in a common cause.

Note: The pamphlet *So You've Been Asked To . . . Chair a Committee* by Jeff Stam (CRC Publications, 1999) identifies seven characteristics of an effective leader and discusses the practical side of chairing a committee. Stam calls a church committee a microcosm of the body of Christ. "Like the brain, your function as chairperson is to manage, track, coordinate, be alert to malfunctions, and suggest corrective action for all the other parts. The brain, however, cannot speak, act, or engage in ministry in any way without the whole body working together."

3. **A working group needs to have a clear idea of its task and develop a set of goals to guide its work.**

This third key principle for building community within your group is closely related to the congregation's vision. Clearly defined expectations and goals give members a sense of security and purpose.

The education committee at Hope Community Church has been charged with overseeing Hope's education program from preschool children to senior adults. This includes the Sunday morning church school program and a variety of midweek groups. It does not include teen club and youth group, which are guided by the youth council.

Hope's education committee recently reviewed its written goals and policies to make sure that they promote the congregation's new mission statement. As a result of this review, the committee realized it needs to offer two new programs: one to train and equip members for outreach and another that will draw in those who are curious about Christianity. The committee has added these two programs to its list of goals for this year.

Once your group has reviewed your congregation's mission and vision statement, take a look at your working group's goals. If you don't have specific written goals, discuss and write down what those goals might be. (You may be surprised at the diversity of opinion about your direction!) Then decide as a group which goals you will attempt to achieve in the next year (or within the time-frame your group will function). Deliberately determine how these goals mesh with the mission and vision statements. Write them down, and make sure every member has a copy. Review them periodically to see if your work is on target.

4. Individual members of a working small group need to decide together and commit to how their group will operate.

This fourth principle for building community into your group focuses on each member's ownership of and commitment to the group's ministry. Conflict, misunderstanding, and antagonism can result when members within a task group have different understandings about the relative importance of their varied tasks.

What happens when Jacob, a member of Hope's education committee, believes that administering the committee's budget is its most important task, while Mary Ruth believes that teacher recruitment should top the list? Meanwhile Susan wishes she could stir up a passion for education within the church and thinks this may be what the committee should focus on first.

Much of this kind of conflict can be avoided when members take the time to discuss and agree on the structure and parameters of their group. Small group experts call this agreement a "covenant" because it expresses commitment to the other members of the group while keeping its focus on God at the center.

"Hidden agendas undermine a group and keep it from functioning effectively. Some expectations are unconscious and remain so unless group members are encouraged to explore them. A 'contract discussion' [or covenant] allows for that exploration" (Julie Gorman, *Community That Is Christian: A Handbook on Small Groups,* p. 134).

The covenant that a group develops should outline the purpose of the group and the responsibilities of each member in accomplishing this purpose. It might include such points as how often and how long the group meets, schedule and location details, leadership, and perhaps even child-care arrangements. It should also include how it will evaluate itself and a commitment to confidentiality, regular attendance, and accountability. (We've included an example of a group covenant on p. 24.)

5. A working group needs to practice sound management principles in its operation.

If you want your group members to be enthusiastic and committed and maintain high morale, it's important to run a good meeting. (We've included a sample planning sheet on p. 25). Good meetings involve many factors: sound planning; a prepared, written agenda; members who do their homework; efficient leaders who focus on essential matters and keep the meeting running on time; and a good balance between discussion and decision making.

Community building and efficient meetings are not mutually exclusive. In fact, a well-run meeting allows more time for individuals to build relationships and support each other through prayer and listening. A well-planned and executed meeting gives members confidence that they're accomplishing what they set out to do and shows them that the leader values their precious time.

GROWING INTO LEADERSHIP

So you find yourself the leader of your working group. Perhaps you or others have just recently identified your gifts of leadership and administration through a formal process such as *Discover Your Gifts* (see pp. 17 and 136). Or maybe your gift of leadership in the workplace or in other ministries in your church and community have been recognized.

Whether you are veteran leader or this is your first experience, you can grow in your leadership role. You'll find practical help for church leaders in the *So You've Been Asked To . . . Lead a Small Group; . . . Chair a Committee; . . . Recruit Volunteers* pamphlets published by CRC Publications. Another good resource is *Working Together: Leading a Task-Oriented Small Group* by Dan Poffenberger, Judy Stack Nelson, and Patrick Keifert.

When your working small group follows these five key principles, you will be well on the way toward moving beyond your agenda and building community. Next we'll look at activities that build relationships within your group.

SMALL GROUP COVENANT

A small group covenant is a set of ground rules that helps to establish boundaries and encourage members' perception that the group is a safe place. These rules may vary, but they should be discussed and developed by the members. The following are some ideas to consider in developing your small group's covenant.

1. The reason our group exists is

2. Our specific group goals include

3. We meet _____ time(s) a month, and this covenant will be in effect for _____ weeks/months. At the end of the covenant period, we will evaluate our progress and growth.

4. We will meet on _____ (day of week) from _____ to _____ (meeting time).

5. Our meetings will be held at _____ (location).

6. We agree to the following group disciplines (choose one or more):

   - Attendance—We will be here whenever possible. This group will be a priority. We will let the group know if we will be late or unable to attend.
   - Ownership—We agree to share responsibility for the group and our goals.
   - Confidentiality—We agree to keep here whatever is shared here.
   - Accountability—We give each other permission to hold us accountable for the goals we set.
   - Accessibility—We give one another permission to call when there is a need.

7. Our plan for service and outreach (to the church, our neighborhood, our community, and so on) needs to be discussed and developed. Written minutes can serve as part of the contract.

8. Other possible ground rules:

   - Food and snacks (Who's responsible for bringing what?)
   - Child care
   - Group leadership (Will there be a single leader with an apprentice, or rotating leadership?)
   - A plan for growth and eventual multiplication into two groups (if this is an option)

—Adapted from Thom Corrigan, *Experiencing Community: A Pilgrimage Small Group Guide* (pp. 37-38). Used by permission.

SAMPLE MEETING PLANNER

Location: _____

Opening Time: _____

Closing Time: _____

Pre-meeting set-up details:

- Where are you in terms of reaching the goals your working small group has set?

- How will you build relationships in this meeting?

- Are there faith issues that need addressing? Do any of your goals and tasks need a faith perspective? How will you address this?

- Do any of your group members have special needs that can be addressed through the group?

Time	Goals for this time	Person responsible	Resources needed
Part 1			
Part 2			
Part 3			
Part 4			

—Poffenberger, Nelson, Keifert, *Working Together: Leading a Task-Oriented Small Group* (p. 11). Used by permission.

- The devotions in Part Two of this book are designed to help you deal with relational, faith, and special needs issues. You'll want to allow twenty minutes for this part of the meeting.

It's All About Love—and Seating Plans

What's the usual agenda for your working group meeting? If yours is like most, your meeting will start with prayer, perhaps a song or some Scripture reading, and a short meditation. This will take about five minutes of your precious time, and then you'll move on . . . and on . . . and on . . . until the closing prayer puts an end to it all.

Where do you usually meet for these marathons? Is the room small and stuffy, or are you the favored ones who get the church parlor with sofas? Perhaps you meet around a long, narrow table, or, if your working group is the worship team, you stand around on the podium. You may have access to a piano, chalkboard, or overhead projector—or maybe none of these.

What's the level of communication in your group? Possibly your group begins with some small talk about the weather and then buckles down to the agenda. If you spend time on a member's personal needs during the meeting, you may feel that you've gotten off track. And as for more serious prayer—that would probably take too much time.

To move beyond the agenda, you'll want to consider all of these factors—routines, seating plans, meeting space, discussion, prayer—and more. This chapter looks at ten things that can have a significant effect on the sense of community within your group and offers practical suggestions for building relationships in your working group meetings.

Physical Group Dynamics

Three aspects of physical group dynamics play an important part in building community within your group. When looking for a place to meet, consider these three Ss:

- **Space.** Fascinating studies have been done to determine the comfort zone of people in groups. Females feel more comfortable in a crowded room than males do. People who feel too crowded sometimes become irritable and respond negatively to each other. The closer a relationship, the more comfortable people are sitting close to each other. Since your aim is to build relationships, you will want to make sure that people are seated within a comfortable social distance of four to twelve feet; a public distance of more than twelve feet between any two people will discourage community building.
- **Seating.** The circle seating arrangement where people can see each other when they speak is most conducive to communication. Sitting in a row, such as three people sitting together on a sofa, presents the most difficult communication arrangement. People in corners or those who sit behind others speak out less. While helpful for taking notes, sitting around a table—often with the leader at the end—discourages intimacy. You may want to move away from the tables for the devotional part of your meeting.
- **Size.** The number of potential relationships within a group multiplies with each new member, a factor that can discourage close relationships. The ideal size of a group for discussion is five people; in any group over eight, there will likely be people who do not contribute at all. Of course, larger groups will appeal to those who don't want high involvement; they also provide a larger pool of gifts, knowledge, and abilities. To encourage greater intimacy in larger task groups, subdivide into smaller clusters during sharing times.

—Gorman, *Community That Is Christian* (pp. 129-133)

Self-disclosure

Self-disclosure, letting people know who you are, is essential for building trust and intimacy. "In order to see, I have to be willing to be seen. If a man takes off his sunglasses I can hear him better" (Hugh Prather in Gorman's *Community That Is Christian: A Handbook on Small Groups*, p. 139). Ideally, when people understand each other enough to empathize with them, an atmosphere of acceptance and appreciation prevails in a working group.

Pastor Roberta Hestenes tells what happened when she suggested that a church board include a community-building sharing time in every meeting. "I was told it would never work. . . . We had hassles and hassles and more hassles. But we started a time of sharing and the Session meetings actually dropped in length. The warmth and quality in the meeting improved. . . . It was just amazing. When people felt cared for, they could participate in a different way" (*Turning Committees into Communities*, p. 29).

Dropping our mask so people can see the real us also carries with it the risk of rejection. Thus we may resist revealing very much about ourselves, fearing that self-disclosure will make us vulnerable. That is why it pays to spend proportionately more time in the beginning of the life of your working group building relationships. "We become a team only after we have discovered who we are as individuals in relation to others in the group" (Gorman, *Community That Is Christian: A Handbook on Small Groups*, p. 142). Taking that extra time to get to know each other is not wasted time.

Opportunities to share can take many forms. Sharing in smaller groups is less stressful than in large groups (the more people you reveal yourself to, the more risk you are taking). The easiest and safest kind of information to share with each other is factual (occupation, marital status, favorite relaxation, taste in music, and so on). Reminiscing about past or present incidents or talking about future hopes and dreams can also be a nonthreatening way of revealing information about yourself.

Sharing questions and other relational activities are included in the devotional exercises found later in this book. (We've included a few sample "icebreaker" questions in the box on p. 30.) Don't skip these community-building activities—they're just as important as your agenda.

Communication

The members of Hope's education committee communicate with each other in a multitude of different ways. Remember John, the member who came late to the meeting? His posture, appearance, and movements could have told the other members a lot before he ever opened his mouth to explain his tardiness. Imagine what any one of these scenarios might have communicated:

- John rushes into the room, his face flushed and his eyes flashing.
  (On his way to church, did John have a fender-bender?)
- John tiptoes into the room, making no eye contact, head and shoulders slumped.
  (John's down. Things at work and home aren't going well, and he wonders why he's even bothered to come to this meeting.)
- John's face is wreathed in a smile a mile wide, and he's full of energy.
  (John's wife gave birth to their first child earlier that day, and he's been on the phone telling everyone the good news.)

Communication is a complex process. Researchers estimate that only seven percent of our communication depends on the words we speak; the rest of our message comes through our body language and the tone we use when we speak. Sighs, frowns, nods, gestures, and facial expressions are all nonverbal forms of communication.

Verbal communication happens on two levels: the information or facts we give and the underlying meaning attached to those facts. Because of the emotions and background of both sender and receiver, misunderstanding happens even when the words we speak are factually correct. "Being aware of these factors and not labeling them with more weight than they deserve is a first step in improving communication. We will never have perfect understanding. . . . Being in community is a call to commit oneself to the work and time required to develop healthy interpersonal communication—not to enter a community where there is no miscommunication" (Gorman, *Community That Is Christian: A Handbook on Small Groups,* p. 188).

Listening

There are two halves to communicating: speaking and listening. In any situation involving more than two people, if each member is an equal participant, people will spend more time listening than speaking. Yet little formal training is available for this most important skill.

Probably the biggest problem in a small group is that while people may give an impression that they are listening, they are in fact focusing on what they want to say when it is their turn to speak. Using some of the techniques found in the box on p. 32 can help you foster good listening skills within your group. (We've incorporated these and other group-building listening skills into the devotions in Part Two of this book.)

Affirmation

Becoming part of a close group can be a wonderful support; but it can also be a scary proposition. People may wonder if they are giving up their individuality in order to be part of the larger body. So it is important to affirm every person's uniqueness and appreciate the gifts that each one brings to make the body of Christ stronger.

31

SMALL GROUP LISTENING SKILLS

To strengthen listening skills, try these techniques in your working groups:

- Have partners talk to each other, then share each other's information with the larger group.

- Suggest that members listen for specific information. For example, in a discussion about finances, listen for a practical way to save money or improve the bottom line.

- Ask clarifying questions such as, Could you explain what you meant when you said . . . ? I'm not sure I understand your (terminology, stance, concern, or . . .).

- Give permission to enjoy silence. It can take time to formulate answers, consider opinions, evaluate what you've heard. By encouraging members to reflect before they talk, the quality of your discussion will improve.

- Draw quiet people into the discussion by soliciting their input.

- Model attentive posture with good eye contact and receptive body language.

- Listen for the feelings beneath the words, and then respond to the feelings you hear with an "I" statement ("I sense that you're feeling . . . about . . . ").

- Prevent a few people from dominating the conversation. If this is a problem in your group, ask the group to establish a ground rule about the acceptable frequency of expressing opinions and ideas.

- Summarize what you've heard the group express before saying what you want to say.

Note: Additional verbal and nonverbal communication strategies are suggested in the pamphlet *So You've Been Asked To . . . Lead A Small Group* by Willy Nywening (CRC Publications, 1998). Eye contact, touch, and tone of voice are some of the ways you can communicate a sense of community in your group.

Consider all the ways your working group members are different. Some are thinkers; others lead from the heart. Some are introverted; others are outgoing. Some are good at administration; others excel at interpersonal skills. Some are people of habit and routine; others are flexible and creative.

It's part of the sinful human condition to be self-centered, to think that our own way of doing and approaching things is the best way, the right way. But Scripture teaches something totally different. When group members are accepted for who they are as part of the body of Christ, their basic needs of belonging and feeling loved will be met. (We've given you some ways to convey this acceptance in the box below.)

PRACTICING AFFIRMATION

- Give genuine, positive feedback to every person in your group every time you meet. Be generous with verbal praise and appreciation for a creative idea, a mundane task performed, a loving correction, a specific gift, a helping hand.

- Encourage open communication and constructive criticism. Before verbally criticizing someone's suggestion, say two positive things about it.

- Apportion each task to the person who has the gifts to accomplish it. The person with the gift of hospitality, for instance, could host your group meetings; someone with the gift of encouragement could be in charge of writing thank-you notes and cards.

Worship

Our worship of God directs our service to each other. That simple spiritual principle can make a big difference in your working group dynamics. When group members really worship together, they are brought into God's presence. From that position, they will have a different perspective on relationships, problems, tasks, and decisions.

This principle is consistent with the greatest commandment: "Love the Lord your God with all your heart and with all your soul and with all your mind" (Matt. 22:37). God's love for us and our love for God strengthens and motivates us. Then, and only then, are we able to keep the second commandment: "Love your neighbor as yourself" (v. 39).

But how does this principle play out in our working small group meetings? When Hope's education committee meets, they begin and end with prayer. And that's good. But there could be more, much more. Worship "turns our thoughts and attention totally to God and being honest—letting him know how much we love and adore him for who he is" (Thom Corrigan, *Experiencing Community: A Pilgrimage Small Group Guide*).

We can focus on God in different ways. Reading appropriate Scripture passages and meditating on them, singing, using silence as a time for reflection and meditation, sharing favorite Scripture passages, and praying together are a few ways to bring a group into the presence of God. (You'll find these and other ideas for worship in Part Two of this book.)

Sometimes the short amount of time available for worship and community building may inhibit genuine worship. Instead of including a short time of worship in every meeting, you may want to devote a complete meeting occasionally to worship or have a longer time of worship built into specific meetings. The times your group devotes to worshiping God are sacred times that do much to build the body and inspire and challenge members for future service.

Prayer

It's common practice to open and close a meeting with prayer, asking for blessings and wisdom and giving thanks. But we can pray together in so many other ways.

The more your group prays together, the closer you will grow as a community, and the more you will be able to discern God's will for your work. Few would dispute this spiritual truth, but fewer still practice it within their groups. Prayer often gets squeezed out by the "tyranny of the urgent."

To make prayer a priority within your working small group, members need to commit to prayer, holding each other accountable and scheduling it as the most important part of your agenda. It's as simple—and as difficult—as that.

Prayer is a prominent feature of the devotions in this book. You may be introduced to ways of praying that are new to some or all of the members in your group. (We've described three creative ideas in the box below). These ways of praying may feel awkward; but just as we express ourselves to other people in many ways, so we can listen to God and express ourselves to God in many ways that will broaden our horizons and increase our joy.

PRAYER IDEAS

Challenge your group to participate in some of the following ideas for prayer:

Prayer Vigils
A vigil is a concentrated effort by a number of believers who commit to praying for specific needs for a designated length of time. (Believers prayed round the clock for Peter when he was imprisoned.)

Prayerwalking
Individually or in small groups, people walk through a chosen geographic area, stopping to pray for the specific needs of that location. A prayer walk can cover the church, with stops in each room to pray for the activities that happen there, or it can include the church's neighborhood, with stops at the homes of each neighbor to pray for those who live there.

Concert of Prayer
Individuals gather to pray under the direction of one or more leaders; individual prayers on named topics blend to offer a single prayer to God. Prayer is interspersed with music and Bible reading as God also speaks to the people.

—Alvin J. Vander Griend with Edith Bajema,
The Praying Church Sourcebook (pp. 1, 21, 30)

Confidentiality

Your working group needs to be a safe place to discuss, disclose, share, solve problems, and even occasionally vent. If confidential information about what happens in your group becomes generally available, it will be difficult to build trust among members.

Your group may not have a written covenant covering operational details, but at a minimum, you should come to an understanding about confidentiality. A discussion within your group will likely reveal that people have many different interpretations of confidentiality. For some it means no disclosure to anyone outside the group about anything that happens within the group. For others it means that only people-sensitive issues are kept within the group. Your group needs to agree on a definition and then hold each other accountable to it.

A WORKING DEFINITION

Confidentiality: Anything of a personal nature that is said in the meeting is never repeated outside the meeting.

Food

Jesus roasted fish on the beach with his disciples. He fed five thousand hungry listeners on a hillside and attended a wedding in Cana. Scripture is full of stories about people who socialize and eat together. And food is a prominent feature in our own celebrations, family get-togethers, and social gatherings.

Your working group deserves to celebrate and enjoy fellowship, and food can bring people around the table. An occasional potluck supper meeting, a coffee-and-cake intermission, a thermos of coffee and a plate of donuts, or a spread of appetizers greeting early arrivals are all surefire ways of building community in your small group.

Celebration

Your working small group has duties and tasks to perform. Often, getting through your agenda and reaching your goals is a reward in itself. You feel satisfied that the work is completed. End of story.

But your group is also a community of believers. God has given each member various gifts and resources to do these tasks. What better way to say thanks than to celebrate God's grace? The Bible, particularly the Old Testament, tells many stories of gigantic celebrations after tasks were completed. Think of the dance at the edge of the Red Sea, the huge service at the dedication of Solomon's temple and again after Ezra and Nehemiah supervised the restoration of the destroyed temple. Praising God was an integral part of these communal celebrations.

Holding celebrations outside the normal place of meeting (at retreat centers, sanctuaries, restaurants, or auditoriums, for instance), sets them off as special times. Celebrations can include picnics, dinner outings, a worship service, a party, or a weekend away.

Find reasons to celebrate: new members, members departing after contributing to the group, a specific goal successfully accomplished, the end of a season, the launch of a new program. All of these can be the focus of a thankful celebration that encourages the building of relationships within your group.

We've touched on a number of factors that can encourage community building in your working small group. It really is all about love—and seating plans—and the list goes on. And it's about building community while building the kingdom of God.

Down to the Nitty-Gritty—Doing It!

W anting to develop your working group into a community is one thing. Actually doing it is quite another. It may seem as impossible as moving the proverbial mountain, especially if that mountain has been a major feature of your church's landscape. "That's the way we've always done it" and "Yes, but . . . " are major roadblocks to change. But it can be done!

We'll describe three ministry-tested models that show how you can incorporate activities into your working group's agenda that build relationships without blowing up the whole structure and starting from scratch!

The Train Model

This model is presented with permission of Eldean Kamp, who developed and suggested it for Diaconal Ministries in Eastern Canada. (We've adapted it for the devotions in Part Two.) Eldean writes:

> Our diaconate is a small group. It is a place where we "practice" what it means to minister and to receive ministry. It is here we can be ourselves, where we belong or find a caring community, and where we are able to do the work of ministry for and with each other. God uses this as a training

base from which we can learn to minister to those in our congregation and community.

The relationships in our meetings can be enhanced by setting an agenda which will strengthen our intimacy with God and each other, which will develop our caring and sharing as well as accomplish the ministry task to which we are called. Our agenda could be thought of as a train.

Each part of this train is necessary in an agenda in order for us to be and deliver God's love. Each part will help us understand and build an intimate new community.

—"Growing a Community of Deacons,"*Diaconal Ministries in Eastern Canada Newsletter,* February 1999 (pp. 1-2)

A typical two-hour session will have these four train components:

Gathering Time (5-7 minutes)
This time creates an open atmosphere at the beginning of each meeting. It could begin with an icebreaker question: What do you enjoy most about this work? or What meaningful task have you accomplished since we last met?

Prayer and the Word (15-20 minutes)
Either the chair or an assigned person leads in a time of devotion that includes an opening prayer, a Scripture passage, and/or some devotional thoughts. The readings should speak to some part of the work you are currently doing. A time of sharing through questions, discussion, and prayer follows.

Ministry Task (90 minutes)
This will take up the biggest part of the agenda. Keeping your working group's goals and purposes in mind, you'll identify major issues, give progress reports, solve problems, and assign tasks. These are the tracks that keep your working group moving forward.

Caring and Prayer (15 minutes)
Of course you care for each other throughout the agenda. But this is a time designated to share ministry and personal concerns and to pray for each other and for the needs that have been highlighted throughout the session.

Willow Creek Small Group Model

This large, seeker-targeted church in the suburbs of Chicago aims to connect each member to a small group. "Connecting people in a small group is not an optional sub-ministry of the church—it *is* the church in its smallest unit. . . . A variety of small groups are necessary to meet the individual needs of believers as well as the diverse needs of the body as a whole. People can grow in Christ-likeness, care for each other, and make a contribution in any group, whether it be a disciple-making group, task group, nurture group . . . " (*Willow Creek Small Groups Leadership Handbook*, p. 7).

Small groups at Willow Creek, no matter what their focus, share these four common components:

- Love (John 13:34-35)
- Learn (Matt. 11:29)
- Decide (Acts 6:1-6)
- Do (James 2:17)

At Willow Creek, various groups spend different proportions of their meeting time engaged in these activities. For instance, a grief support ministry group would devote half of its meeting time to the love component; learning, deciding, and doing would take up the rest of the time. On the other hand, a food service group would spend half of its agenda on doing; an elders group would devote half of its agenda to deciding; while a seekers Bible study group would spend proportionately more time on learning.

Using this model, the education committee at Hope Community Church might focus on the deciding component. Their two-hour agenda might look something like this:

- *Love (5-10 minutes)*
  The initial gathering time is used to find out what's been going on in everyone's life since the last meeting, perhaps through a sharing question. Love is shown through listening, expressing concern, and encouragement.

- *Learn (20 minutes)*
  This part of the meeting is devoted to the study and discussion of a passage of Scripture, devotional readings, or readings from various leaders in church education. A devotional reading might focus on God's call to Moses to lead the Israelites out of Egypt. In discussing this call to leadership, Hope's committee

members realize that good teachers also need a sense of calling, and this will influence how they carry out their recruitment strategy.

- *Decide (60 minutes)*
  The group takes care of agenda items that need attention. It refers to its goals and ministry statements to make decisions about budgeting, recruiting, and how to respond to an irate volunteer. These decisions ultimately will benefit the church education programs in the church and build up God's kingdom.

- *Do (10 minutes)*
  The group brainstorms changes that could be made to the education program to deal with the volunteer's concerns. The secretary is asked to draft an amendment to the group's policies and include a copy with the minutes to be mailed to members.

- *Love (10 minutes)*
  Yolanda, the chairperson, invites members to reflect on the decisions of the evening, and also asks for prayer requests, both personal and group-related. John may reveal that he's having difficulty keeping up with his committee work because of the turmoil in his personal life.

- *Do (10 minutes)*
  Mary Ruth volunteers to relieve John of some of his recruiting calls so he'll have more time for his family. The evening ends in prayer as members pray for the various concerns expressed.

Evergreen Baptist Church Model

In her book *Community That Is Christian: A Handbook on Small Groups* (pp. 304-306), Gorman gives another suggestion for organizing your working group agenda, using Evergreen Baptist Church in Rosemead, California, as an example. All of the small groups at Evergreen incorporate the following elements into their meetings:

- Missions and Ministry
- Nurture and Worship
- Community
- Training

Following this model, Hope's education committee meeting might look like this:

- *Nurture and Worship (20 minutes)*
  The group sings, prays, focuses on Scripture, reflects, rejoices, and praises God. (The devotions in Part Two could be used for this purpose.)

- *Training (20 minutes)*
  The group views a video on recruitment and reads through and reviews guidelines for budgeting as outlined in their policy manual.

- *Missions and Ministry (60 minutes)*
  The business of the committee—budget, recruitment, and an irate letter from a volunteer—takes up the largest portion of time. After members agree on a strategy for recruitment, Gerald and Mary Ruth agree to work together with the church education superintendent for this purpose. Jacob agrees to bring a concrete proposal on budget changes to the next meeting. Members brainstorm changes to the education program and make decisions on how and when to implement them.

- *Community (20 minutes)*
  The group reflects on its work in an open-ended discussion. Yolanda asks members if they have any concerns about their assigned tasks or anything in their personal lives that might affect their ability to do their tasks. She asks that each person choose an accountability partner, so that each can encourage and challenge the other. The meeting ends with a "popcorn prayer" in which short, specific petitions and reasons for thanksgiving are prayed by individual members.

All of these models incorporate the classic agenda, while placing more emphasis on elements that can transform your working group into a unified community of believers. Your group may choose a format with different labels, but your meeting agenda should include time to grow in your relationship with God and each other right along with time for service. The church—the body of Christ—is sure to benefit from a renewed emphasis on love, caring, sharing, and seeking God's will through prayer and study of the Word.

Part Two:

Devotions for the Working Small Group

How to Use These Devotions

For Your Meetings

We've designed the twenty-eight devotions in this book to help your group move beyond the working agenda during your regular meetings. Devotions are grouped into these three categories:

- Called to Lead (Devotions 1-10)
- Called to Serve (Devotions 11-19)
- Called Together (Devotions 20-28)

Specific elements of each devotion include the following:

- Build Community
- Open God's Word
- Reflect on the Word
- Live Out the Word
- Pray Together

Depending on the model you choose for your meeting (see pp. 39-43), you'll need to decide where these five elements will be placed within your agenda. It's important to schedule a time to build community early in your meeting. Doing so signals that spending time together with God as a community of believers is the first priority of your life and of your meetings.

Most of the time, all you'll need to lead this part of your meeting is this book. Here are some things you'll want to note as you plan your meetings:

- Scripture passages are written out in full. (We've used the NIV unless another version is noted. You may want to have Bibles available for each member.)
- At least one song title is suggested for each devotion. You'll find a list of these songs in the back of this book (pp. 145-146). Sometimes the text is included in the devotion so that you can read the words or sing them without the printed music. Most of the music for these songs can be found in hymnals and songbooks.
- Occasionally you may want to photocopy group discussion questions, activities, or song texts to encourage more group participation.
- You may want to write group responses on an overhead, blackboard, or chart for some sessions.
- Visual aids will enhance your time together, but these are left to your own creative ingenuity.

Because working groups have busy agendas, all of the devotions are timed to fit into a twenty-minute time slot. (You'll have to stick closely to the suggested schedule to stay within this time limit.) While members will appreciate your commitment to staying within time limits, once they've experienced the benefits of a relationship-building component in their meetings, they may want to extend the discussion or worship times. In fact, we hope that's what will happen. Let the Spirit of God guide you in deciding the balance of time your group spends on business and building relationships.

For Leadership Retreats

You may want to use these devotions to lead an all-day or weekend retreat at the beginning or middle of a church season. By extending the group activities and the time of worship and prayer, each session could be expanded to an hour or more. Or use specific devotions to introduce a task if your retreat is focusing on planning the church year. For instance, "A Vision of a Better Future" (devotion 3, pp. 58-60) could introduce a vision-casting session.

Other possibilities include organizing a retreat with the theme of leadership around the first devotion found in each of the three sections of the book (Called to Lead, Called to Serve, and Called Together) or focusing on one aspect of leadership, using three or four devotions to build your meetings around that theme (We've included a suggested plan for a leadership retreat in the boxes on pp. 50-51).

Singing in a small group may feel a bit awkward at first if you have no instrument to accompany you. Here are some ideas to help you incorporate singing into your small group:

- Have everyone hum the melody while someone reads the text of the song.

- Sing only one phrase of a song as a short prayer refrain. For example, to introduce or conclude your spoken prayers, sing together only the first line of "Breathe on Me, Breath of God" or "Spirit of the Living God."

- Play a recording of the suggested songs or other songs to accompany your time of prayer and reflection.

Note: You must obtain permission from the publisher to photocopy the text and music of copyrighted songs. We've generally included the publisher's address in the credit line.

THE JOYS OF LEADERSHIP RETREAT

This four-session retreat plan could be carried out on a Friday night and Saturday. You may want to add a session to introduce your working small group's mission, develop goals for the year, discuss job descriptions, and so on. Keep in mind, though, that the main purpose of your retreat is to build community in a group of people called by God.

Session 1: Called by God
40 minutes plus worship time

Devotion 1: The Calling (pp. 52-54)
Spend the first twenty minutes having group members tell how they came to be part of the group. Encourage them to share what gifts they feel they bring to the group and what concerns they have about serving in this ministry.

Read aloud the Scripture passage (Ex. 3:6-14) and the meditation (Open God's Word and Reflect on the Word). Allow twenty to thirty minutes instead of ten for the small and large group questions (Live Out the Word).

The worship time (Pray Together) can be as long as you like. This is a time for group members to commit themselves to the group's calling. You may wish to ask a worship team to lead this part of your session.

Session 2: Called Together
60-70 minutes

Devotion 20: A Community of Diversity (pp. 114-116)
Begin this session by reading aloud the Scripture passage about the prophets and teachers in Antioch (Acts 13:1-3) and reflect on how God called this diverse group to minister (Open the Word and Reflect on the Word). Spend about a half hour learning more about each other (Live Out the Word). Allow about a half hour for group prayer for each other's needs. Consider including prayers for personal needs, corporate needs, and prayers of commitment in your prayer time. Intersperse these with songs that fit the theme.

Session 3: Called to Lead
90 minutes

Devotion 2: Without a Leader? (pp. 55-57)
Begin this session with a time of worship and fellowship, perhaps singing together around a piano or with guitar accompaniment for about twenty minutes. Then use the Build Community exercise on page 55. Be sure to have Leighton Ford's definition of leadership printed on a chalkboard or overhead so everyone can see it. Allow about ten minutes to discuss the questions.

Read aloud the passage from Exodus 27 (Open God's Word). Allow about ten minutes for the Reflect on the Word section. Draw word pictures of what the Israelites would have been like without Moses or Joshua. Reflect on the Spirit's work in Joshua's life and his reliance on the priest, and praise God for the Spirit's work in qualifying your group members and for our direct access to Jesus, our high priest.

Return to Ford's definition of leadership. Lead the group in a thirty- to forty-minute individual assessment of your working group using these questions: Where are we now? Where should we be? Where do we want to be? Use the prayer prompts (Pray Together) to end this session.

Session 4: Called to Serve
90 minutes

Devotion 11: The *Same* Attitude (pp. 85-88)
Read aloud the Scripture reading and meditation (Open God's Word and Reflect on the Word). Allow at least thirty minutes for group members to complete and discuss the attitude self-assessment (Live Out the Word). Be sure to make a photocopy of the assessment for each group member in advance.

Share answers to the third question with the whole group. Ask group members to talk about the two best ways they feel they can serve in your working group, based on their individual gifts, available time and energy, and the needs of the ministry. Encourage group members to affirm and encourage each other during this exercise.

End your retreat with a time of praise and worship.

Note: If your group members have never completed an inventory of their gifts, you may want to include this as part of your retreat. The course *Discover Your Gifts* by Alvin Vander Griend includes a "Spiritual Gift Discovery Questionnaire" you may find helpful. An abbreviated questionnaire is included on page 136 from the youth version of *Discover Your Gifts* by Ruth Vander Zee. Both courses are available from CRC Publications.

Devotion One

The Calling

Build Community
5 minutes

Have group members explain how they became involved in the ministry of your working group. You'll probably find that some aren't sure why. Others may have had their arm twisted and are reluctant to become involved; still others are eager to use specific gifts.

Open God's Word
2 minutes

Moses never intended to get involved in ministry. One minute he was minding his own business, tending his father-in-law's sheep. Then God spoke to him from a burning bush and his whole life was turned upside down.

"I am the God of your father, the God of Abraham, the God of Isaac and the God of Jacob." At this, Moses hid his face, because he was afraid to look at God.

The LORD said, "I have indeed seen the misery of my people in Egypt. . . . So I have come down to rescue them from the hand of the Egyptians and to bring them up out of that land into a good and spacious land, a land flowing with milk and honey. . . . So now, go. I am sending you to Pharaoh to bring my people the Israelites out of Egypt."

But Moses said to God, "Who am I, that I should go to Pharaoh and bring the Israelites out of Egypt?"

And God said, "I will be with you. And this will be a sign to you that it is I who have sent you: When you have brought the people out of Egypt, you will worship God on this mountain."

Moses said to God, "Suppose I go to the Israelites and say to them, 'The God of your fathers has sent me to you,' and they ask me, 'What is his name?' Then what shall I tell them?"

God said to Moses, "I AM WHO I AM. This is what you are to say to the Israelites: 'I AM has sent me to you.'"

—Exodus 3:6-14

Reflect on the Word

2 minutes

Some people are called to ministry in a dramatic way. Certainly, Moses, Samuel, Isaiah, Paul, and John had no doubts that God was choosing them for a special ministry. But for most people, the call is muffled and confusing. Abraham didn't get a map and a guidebook when he left his homeland. David was anointed king when he was still a shepherd boy, but he waited many long, hard years before his call was fulfilled.

You too have received a call to lead. Perhaps it was a dramatic calling. More likely, you are part of this working group because of a genuine desire to do God's will, influenced by your life experiences, training, interests, and abilities. That too is a calling.

A sense of calling is essential if you are to fulfill your ministry in the kingdom. God has a purpose for your church, and you are part of God's plan to work out that purpose. Sounds like serious business, doesn't it? Like Moses, you may be tempted to say, "Who am I, that God should be counting on me?"

God's answer to you is the same as it was to Moses: "I will be with you." Your working group is called to do God's work, and God will be with you and your group—that's a promise.

When Moses asked, "Who are you?" God's answer was very simple and most profound: "I AM WHO I AM." The great I AM, who was and is and ever will be, sent Moses. The great I AM, who is dependable and faithful, also calls you.

Live Out the Word

6-8 minutes

Talk about these questions in groups of two or three:

- Moses was just going about his job of shepherding when he was called. If you were the central character in a modern-day version of this story, what place at your work might be the site of God's appearance?
- Moses hid his face in fear. How would you react if you heard God's voice?
- What image comes to your mind when you hear the name I AM WHO I AM?

Discuss these questions with your whole group:

- How do you react to the idea that you have been called to the tasks your working group is assigned?
- What objections or arguments might you have with God about this calling?
- What blessings do you anticipate from it?

53

Pray Together

3 minutes

Moses was in the presence of God. The ground where he stood was holy ground. His task was a holy calling. We too are in the presence of God and have received a calling.

Silently come before God on your own patch of holy ground. Commit to the Lord the work that your group will be doing and ask God for strength, wisdom, and discernment to complete the tasks well and to God's glory. End your time of silence and commitment with a brief prayer, or sing or say the words of this song:

"Spirit of the Living God"
Spirit of the living God,
  fall afresh on me;
Spirit of the living God,
  fall afresh on me.
Melt me, mold me, fill me,
  use me.
Spirit of the living God,
  fall afresh on me.

Spirit of the living God,
  move among us all;
make us one in heart and
  mind, make us one in love:
humble, caring, selfless, sharing.
Spirit of the living God,
  fill our lives with love.

—St. 1, Daniel Iverson, 1926. © 1935, 1963, Birdwing Music (admin. by EMI Christian Music Publishing, 101 Winners Circle, Brentwood, TN 37024).

—St. 2, Michael Baughen, 1982. © 1982, Hope Publishing Co., 380 S. Main Plaza, Carol Stream, IL 60188. All rights reserved. Used by permission.

Other songs you might choose are "Breathe on Me, Breath of God" or "Lord, Be Glorified" (p. 80). If you're not sure your group will feel comfortable singing, try some of the suggestions on page 49.

Without a Leader?

Build Community
5 minutes

In *Transforming Leadership* (p. 25), Leighton Ford defines a leader as a "person who helps followers to change, to move from where they are to where they should be or where they want to be." Do you agree with Ford? How do you define leadership? (It might help to write the definitions on a chalkboard or overhead. If your group is large, divide into smaller clusters of three or four to discuss the questions.)

Open God's Word
2 minutes

This passage from Exodus provides a good description of what's involved in biblical leadership. It's as applicable today as it was during the time of Moses.

Then the LORD said to Moses, "Go up this mountain in the Abarim range and see the land I have given the Israelites. After you have seen it, you too will be gathered to your people."

Moses said to the LORD, "May the LORD, the God of the spirits of all mankind, appoint a man over this community to go out and come in before them, one who will lead them out and bring them in, so the LORD's people will not be like sheep without a shepherd."

So the LORD said to Moses, "Take Joshua son of Nun, a man in whom is the spirit, and lay your hand on him. Have him stand before Eleazar the priest and the entire assembly and commission him in their presence. Give him some of your authority so the whole Israelite community will obey him. He is to stand before Eleazar the priest, who will obtain decisions for him by inquiring of the Urim before the LORD. At his command he and the entire community of the Israelites will go out, and at his command they will come in."

—Numbers 27:12-13, 15-21

Reflect on the Word
2 minutes

Imagine the Israelites without a leader. Moses shuddered as he contemplated the idea. He knew that they would be like sheep without a shepherd, in danger of falling prey to enemies, hunger, and thirst. God agreed with Moses and called Joshua to become the next leader.

Leadership is necessary, not optional. This means that your working group is necessary too. You've been called to do an important job.

Joshua was chosen by God because the divine spirit was present in him. Having God's Spirit in us is an essential qualification for leadership. After choosing Joshua, God equipped him to do the work; God commissioned Joshua and gave him authority. God will do the same for your group members.

Joshua relied on the priest to inquire of God whenever he needed to make a decision. God directed Joshua and told him what to do. But we don't have to go through a priest for direction. We have Jesus, whom Paul describes as "a high priest, who sat down at the right hand of the throne of the Majesty in heaven, and who serves in the sanctuary" (Heb. 8:1-2).

Jesus is always available to direct us through his Word and to intercede for us before God's throne when we have difficult decisions to make, when we disagree on procedure, when we feel discouraged or lost. We can always rely on him. Praise God!

Live Out the Word
5 minutes

Discuss these questions with your whole group or in groups of two or three:

- Moses described leadership in terms of shepherding. How would you describe the leadership your group provides to your congregation? Are you like

  a general leading an army?

  a manager directing office staff?

  creative thinkers in a computer software firm?

  mountain guides for an Everest expedition?

  bookkeepers at an accounting firm?

  [add your own example.]

- What does your choice say about the style of leadership you are using? What kind of leadership would you like to be using?

56

Pray Together

5-6 minutes

Structure your group prayer around these specific prompts:

- We thank you, God of Moses and Joshua and of [name each one in your group].
- We thank you, God, for equipping us with gifts and resources to do your work. We thank you for [name one gift or resource each person brings to your group].
- Lord, we confess that we stand in need of your help and direction. As we look at our work, we ask you for [name specific needs].

Conclude your prayer time singing or saying the words from one or more of the songs below.

"Lead Me, Guide Me"

*Lead me [us], guide me [us],
  along the way,
for if you lead me [us], I [we]
  cannot stray.
Lord, let me [us] walk each day
  with you,
lead me [us] my [our] whole life
  [lives] through.*

"Lord, Listen to Your Children Praying"

*Lord, listen to your children
  praying,
Lord, send your Spirit in this
  place;
Lord, listen to your children
  praying,
send us love, send us power; send
  us grace!*

"O Master, Let Me Walk with Thee"

*O Master, let me walk with thee
  in lowly paths of service free;
tell me thy secret; help me bear
  the strain of toil, the fret of
  care.*

*In hope that sends a shining ray
  far down the future's
  broadening way,
in peace that only thou canst
  give, with thee, O Master, let
  me live.*

—Washington Gladden, 1879

A Vision of a Better Future

Build Community
2 minutes

Have group members share with a partner about a time when a dream—a desired goal—came true.

Open God's Word
3 minutes

When the people of Israel were close to the promised land, Moses sent a party of spies to check out the place. This is the report of the majority (the ten spies):

"We went into the land to which you sent us, and it does flow with milk and honey! Here is its fruit. But the people who live there are powerful, and the cities are fortified and very large. . . . We can't attack those people; they are stronger than we are."
—Numbers 13:27-28, 31

This is the "minority" report from Caleb and Joshua:

"We should go up and take possession of the land, for we can certainly do it."
—Numbers 13:30

The people chose to listen to the majority.

That night all the people of the community raised their voices and wept aloud. . . . And they said to each other, "We should choose a leader and go back to Egypt."

Then Moses and Aaron fell facedown in front of the whole Israelite assembly gathered there. Joshua son of Nun and Caleb son of Jephunneh, who were among those who had explored the land, tore their clothes and said to the entire Israelite assembly, "The land we passed through and explored is exceedingly good. If the LORD is pleased with us, he will lead us into that land, a land flowing with milk and honey, and will give it to us. Only do not rebel against the LORD. And do not be afraid of the people of the land, because we will swallow them up. Their protection is gone, but the

LORD *is with us. Do not be afraid of them."*

—Numbers 14:1, 4-9

Reflect on the Word
3 minutes

Leaders need to have vision, a clear mental image of the way things could be or should be in the days ahead. That vision is based on an awareness of God's leading and reliance on God's promises.

The twelve spies Moses sent over the Jordan all saw the same thing, but only two of them had vision. They could see past the obstacles because they remembered God's promises. They could picture in their mind's eye the reality of the Israelites conquering Palestine.

This story graphically illustrates the true consequences of lack of vision: "Where there is no vision, the people perish" (Prov. 29:18, KJV). The Israelites chose to listen to the people with no vision, and they died in the wilderness. Only Joshua and Caleb survived to see and experience the reality of God's promises.

Your working group is called to provide leadership to your church as you fulfill a specific task. That implies enormous responsibility: the responsibility to catch God's vision for your group and to steadfastly communicate that vision to those you lead. Sometimes that vision may be unpopular and may seem impossible. But like Joshua and Caleb, you can say, "If the LORD is pleased with us, he will lead us . . . the LORD is with us, do not be afraid."

Live Out the Word
10 minutes

If your church has a vision statement, distribute copies to every member of your group. Together review and affirm your commitment to this vision by discussing these questions:

- Do you understand the scope of the vision statement?
- Do you support the vision wholeheartedly? With reservations?
- How does the work you're currently doing (or have been asked to do) in your group support the vision of the church?
- What changes would you suggest in the vision statement or in your working group?

If your church has no vision statement to serve as the foundation for the work of your small group, it doesn't necessarily mean your group has no vision. The vision may not be formalized in a written statement. It's also possible that the unspoken visions of members of your working group differ from each other's and are causing friction.

On chalkboard, overhead transparency, or chart paper, write the following definition:

> Vision for ministry is a clear mental image of a preferable future imparted by God to his chosen servants, and is based upon an accurate understanding of God, self, and circumstances.

—George Barna, *The Power of Vision* (p. 28)

Have group members write down a one-sentence description of their vision of where the Lord is leading your working group; share the answers verbally. The results could be the grounds for a fruitful discussion and the beginnings of a written vision statement. If you feel the need to continue this exercise, you'll want to devote more time, prayer, and energy to it than these few moments afford. The booklet *Charting a Course for Your Church* (Dirk J. Hart, CRC Publications, 1997) offers basic guidelines for the visioning process.

Pray Together
2 minutes

Spend a minute or two in quiet personal reflection, thinking of times when God's leading was especially evident. Praise God for always leading. Then close your time together with this prayer:

> O God, thank you for your promise to be with us. Be our guide as we explore the vision you have set before our group. Help us to see with your eyes the wonderful future you hold before us, if only we will follow where you lead. Amen.

Or if your group enjoys singing together, use this song as your prayer:

"Lead Me, Guide Me"
Lead me [us], guide me [us], along the way,
for if you lead me [us], I [we] cannot stray.
Lord, let me [us] walk each day with you,
lead me [us] my [our] whole life [lives] through.

Waiting and Listening

Build Community
3 minutes

As fast as you can think of them, list all the ways people communicate with each other today. Include different kinds of verbal, nonverbal, and electronic communication. Think of how technology has reduced the time we wait for a response.

Open God's Word
2 minutes

After his resurrection, Jesus appeared to his disciples over a period of forty days, teaching them about the kingdom of God. Jesus' parting words to his disciples and their response are recorded in Acts 1.

"You will receive power when the Holy Spirit comes on you; and you will be my witnesses in Jerusalem, and in all Judea and Samaria, and to the ends of the earth."

After he said this, he was taken up before their very eyes, and a cloud hid him from their sight.

They were looking intently up into the sky as he was going, when suddenly two men dressed in white stood before them. "Men of Galilee," they said, "why do you stand here looking into the sky? This same Jesus, who has been taken from you into heaven, will come back in the same way you have seen him go into heaven."

Then they returned to Jerusalem. . . . When they arrived, they went upstairs to the room where they were staying. Those present were Peter, John, James and Andrew; Philip and Thomas, Bartholomew and Matthew; James, son of Alphaeus and Simon the Zealot, and Judas son of James. They all joined together constantly in prayer, along with the women and Mary the mother of Jesus, and with his brothers.

—Acts 1:8-14

61

Reflect on the Word

4 minutes

As Jesus disappeared from view, imagine the disciples' thoughts: Wait, don't go yet! What are we supposed to do? You tell us to be your witnesses, but you don't leave us with a ministry plan showing us exactly what to do.

Perhaps you sometimes feel the same way when you are faced with making plans for ministry. You may wish that Jesus could be right here with your working group telling you what to do and how to do it.

Picture the disciples talking to each other and wondering what to do first. (You might want to role-play this scene in your group to get at the initial feeling of the disciples.) Perhaps it was Peter—or maybe John—who first remembered that Jesus told them to stay in Jerusalem until the Holy Spirit arrived. Waiting around Jerusalem and praying must have been very hard for hands-on "doers" like Peter, just as waiting and praying instead of making plans for reaching goals may give your working group members the feeling that they're merely treading water, getting nowhere fast.

As the story of the early church continues in Acts 1 and 2, we see that prayer and listening to God for direction are the very activities that are most necessary before we can launch into ministry. During this time of prayer and waiting, Peter led the believers to choose a replacement for Judas. Some time after the ministry team was complete, God sent his promised gift of the Holy Spirit, and then things really began to happen!

Waiting for God and listening to God's direction is not time wasted; it's putting first things first. After that, God can work out his ministry plans through you.

Living Out the Word

8 minutes

Waiting and listening for God's direction implies that

- God sends a message.
- we receive God's message.

To consider how this process of sending and receiving might work in your group, divide in half to discuss the following questions (share your lists with each other):

- *Group One:* How has God spoken to people in the past? How could God speak to your working group today? Compile a list of past and present ways God speaks.
- *Group Two:* What can we do to ensure that we hear God's message? Compile a list of attitudes and actions that

will help you hear God speaking to you.

Pray Together
3 minutes

Begin with a time of silent prayer, asking God to open your ears and your hearts as you seek to do God's will and carry out your calling. Close your time together by saying or singing this prayer for the Spirit's leading:

"Spirit of the Living God"
Spirit of the living God,
*   fall afresh on me;*
Spirit of the living God,
*   fall afresh on me.*
Melt me, mold me, fill me,
*   use me.*
Spirit of the living God,
*   fall afresh on me.*

Spirit of the living God,
*   move among us all;*
make us one in heart and mind,
*   make us one in love:*
humble, caring, selfless, sharing.
Spirit of the living God, fill our
*   lives with love.*

—St. 1, Daniel Iverson, 1926.
© 1935, 1963, Birdwing Music
(admin. by EMI Christian Music
Publishing, 101 Winners Circle,
Brentwood, TN 37024).

—St. 2, Michael Baughen, 1982.
© 1982, Hope Publishing Co.,
380 S. Main Place,
Carol Stream, IL 60188.
All rights reserved.
Used by permission.

Devotion Five

Taking Responsibility

Build Community
3 minutes

How do you typically respond to a big problem? Invite group members to share their responses to the following suggestions (you may want to make photocopies or a transparency):

- Like an ostrich. I like to hide my head in the sand.
- Like a puppy dog. I wag my tail and jump right in without thinking.
- Like a work horse. Just hitch me to the plow, and show me what to do.
- Like a butterfly. I like to flit about from one thing to the next, doing a little bit here, a little bit there.
- Like a sheep. I'll follow the leader, but don't ask me to come up with big ideas.
- Like a lion. I'll stalk the problem, find its weak spot, and wrestle it down to the ground.
- Like [add your own description].

Open God's Word
3 minutes

Nehemiah is a good model for those who are involved in servant leadership. He worked for King Nebuchadnezzar in Babylon when the Israelites were in exile. One day he received troubling news about his fellow countrymen in Judea. The remnant who had returned to Jerusalem to rebuild the temple (Ezra 1:1-5) were living in disgrace, and Jerusalem lay in ruins. Nehemiah was devastated by the news and poured out his heart to God (Neh. 1:4-11). Then Nehemiah went before the king with a plan.

The king asked me, "Why does your face look so sad when you are not ill? This can be nothing but sadness of heart."

I was very much afraid, but I said to the king, "May the king live forever! Why should my face not look sad when the city where

*my fathers are buried lies in ruins,
and its gates have been destroyed
by fire?"*

*The king said to me, "What is
it you want?"*

*Then I prayed to the God of
heaven, and I answered the king,
"If it pleases the king and if your
servant has found favor in his
sight, let him send me to the city
in Judah where my fathers are
buried so that I can rebuild it."*

*Then the king, with the queen
sitting beside him, asked me,
"How long will your journey take,
and when will you get back?" It
pleased the king to send me; so I
set a time.*

*I also said to him, "If it pleases
the king, may I have letters to the
governors of Trans-Euphrates, so
that they will provide me safe-
conduct until I arrive in Judah?
And may I have a letter to Asaph,
keeper of the king's forest, so he
will give me timber to make
beams for the gates of the citadel
by the temple and for the city wall
and for the residence I will
occupy?" And because the
gracious hand of my God was
upon me, the king granted my
requests.*

—Nehemiah 2:2-8

Reflect on the Word
2 minutes

Nehemiah had a problem. Actually, it wasn't only his problem; it was a problem for all of Israel. Their city, the site of God's temple, was in ruins. And this was a symbol of their life as a nation too. But of all the people who knew about the problem, it seems that only Nehemiah was prepared to act on it.

Nehemiah didn't just recognize the problem, he owned it. He took responsibility for fixing it, for doing what he could to make it right again. Nehemiah exhibited the characteristics of leadership: he had a vision, a mental picture of a better future; he listened to God as he communed with God in prayer; and then he set out to solve the problem.

Nehemiah analyzed what was needed to solve the problem in Jerusalem and developed a detailed plan before he went to seek the king's support for his ideas. Nehemiah's story reminds us that when we rely on God, using the gifts God has given us and expecting God to open opportunities for us, amazing things can happen. It was no accident that Nehemiah was a cupbearer to the king (1:11)!

Live Out the Word
10 minutes

Perhaps you have become aware of problems in your congregation, problems that affect the ministry of your working group. Perhaps, like Nehemiah, you are pouring out your heart to God. So far, so good. But what's the next step?

Together or in groups of two or three, discuss the following questions:

- If Nehemiah were a member of your congregation, what issue might he grieve? (Identify one that affects your working group's ministry.)
- Identify the steps your group could take to resolve the issue. (Try to be as specific as Nehemiah was. Write down your plan.)
- Who or what might become an instrument of God to help your group move toward a solution? (Decide who, how, and when you will present your group's plan.)

Pray Together
2 minutes

Pray this prayer of confession:

Dear Lord, we confess that often we would rather let someone else tackle a diffi-cult problem than do it our-selves. Father, you are that "someone else" who can help us see through a problem and arrive at a solution. We pray for your leadership and insight. May we always, like Nehemiah, be prepared to recognize and use the re-sources you send us. In Jesus name, Amen.

Nehemiah reminded the grieving Israelites that the joy of the Lord was their strength (8:10). Remembering that God can do all things, sing this song:

"The Joy of the Lord Is My Strength"
The joy of the Lord is my strength.
The joy of the Lord is my strength.
The joy of the Lord is my strength.
The joy of the Lord is my strength.

He heals the brokenhearted, and they cry no more.
He heals the brokenhearted, and they cry no more.
He heals the brokenhearted, and they cry no more.
The joy of the Lord is my strength.

He gives me living water, and I
  thirst no more.
He gives me living water, and I
  thirst no more.
He gives me living water, and I
  thirst no more.
The joy of the Lord is my
  strength.

—Based on Nehemiah 8:10.
Alliene G. Vale, © 1971,
His Eye Music/MultiSongs/
The Joy of the Lord Publishing
(all print rights admin. by EMI
Christian Music Publishing,
P.O. Box 5085, Brentwood, TN
37024). Used by permission.

Discerning God's Will

Build Community
3 minutes

"Discernment is a discriminating choice between two or more competing options," says Gordon T. Smith in his book *Listening to God in Times of Choice* (p. 2). Invite group members to share about options that are competing in their life or in their family's life at this time. (If your group members are comfortable enough with each other, have them share personal choices they are wrestling with, and invite input from the rest of the group.)

Open God's Word
2 minutes

Every day working small groups within the church are faced with choices: to build or not to build, to incorporate contemporary or traditional styles of worship, to call this pastor or that one, to support this cause or another. . . . (Spend a minute to review the choices your group will face.)

These decisions have the potential to affect the people in your congregation positively or negatively.

The apostle Paul offers the following words of advice to people who are trying to discern the will of God as they make decisions:

I urge you, brothers, in view of God's mercy, to offer your bodies as living sacrifices, holy and pleasing to God—this is your spiritual act of worship. Do not conform any longer to the pattern of this world, but be transformed by the renewing of your mind. Then you will be able to test and approve what God's will is—his good, pleasing, and perfect will.
—Romans 12:1-2

Reflect on the Word
2 minutes

"When it comes to discernment and effective decision making there are no shortcuts. There is no simple method of finding God's will or making easy decisions" (Smith, *Listening to God in Times of Choice*, p. 25).

But in this passage from Romans, Paul offers three principles for discerning God's will:

- God comes first. *"Offer your bodies as living sacrifices. . . . "* Our ultimate allegiance must be to God. This calls for serious soul-searching. We must be sure that we are not choosing what's good for us, but rather what's best for God's kingdom.
- God's Word guides. *"Be transformed by the renewing of your mind. . . . "* Not only do leaders need to have a listening heart, they must also have a mind informed by Scripture rather than conformed to the values of the world. The role of the Bible in guiding decisions is foundational, for God has revealed himself and his will through the Word. When our minds are tuned by the knowledge of God's Word, we can recognize the voice of the Holy Spirit.
- God's people confirm. *"Test and approve what God's will is. . . . "* We need the checks and balances of living in a community of committed Christians who will help us weigh our decisions. No Christian can be an island. God intends for us to live in community, where we can receive correction, encouragement, and accountability.

Live Out the Word
10 minutes

Choose one or more of the following exercises to strengthen your group's understanding and experience of discernment:

Truth in Advertising?

Ask group members to choose a partner, and give each pair an ad from a magazine or newspaper. Have Bibles available for reference. Ask them to respond to the following discussion questions:

In today's world, with shifting values and norms and an emphasis on personal fulfillment, the church very much needs to discern right from wrong and truth from lies. What message is this ad giving you? Is it the truth or a lie? If it's a lie, what Scriptural truth refutes it?

After the discussion, pray for discernment in dealing with the values of the world and for courage to go against the prevailing culture.

Paul's Principles in Practice

Refer back to the three principles for discernment Paul gives in Romans 12:1-2. Together or in groups of two or three, respond to the following questions:

How have you experienced the truth of these three principles in your own life or in the life of a group you've been part of? What was the choice you faced? How did you or your group practice these three principles?

Respond to the discussion by thanking God for these occasions and asking for continued guidance.

Not So Clear-Cut

Some choices are clear-cut. Others require much thought, prayer, discussion, and discernment. As a whole group, quickly identify the clear-cut choices your working group must make and then define the tougher ones with these questions:

What are the issues your working group (or congregation) is considering that are not so clear-cut? What makes them tougher issues? What answers do you wish you had?

After defining these issues, pray for very specific needs that arose in the discussion.

Pray Together

Close your devotional time with a doxology. *Doxology* comes from the Latin words *doxa* (glory) and *logos* (word). Thus doxology means "a glorifying word," an expression of praise that glorifies God.

Use Paul's doxology to glorify the God of knowledge, judgment, and wisdom:

Oh, the depth of the riches of the wisdom and knowledge of God!
How unsearchable his judgments, and his paths beyond tracing out!
Who has known the mind of the Lord? Or who has been his counselor?
Who has ever given to God, that God should repay him?
For from him and through him and to him are all things.
To him be the glory forever! Amen.
—Romans 11:33-36

You may also want to sing one or both of the doxologies on this and the next page.

"We Will Glorify"
We will glorify the King of kings,
we will glorify the Lamb;
we will glorify the Lord of lords,
who is the great I AM.

Hallelujah to the King of kings,
hallelujah to the Lamb;
hallelujah to the Lord of lords,
who is the great I AM.

"Amen, We Praise Your Name" ("Amen, Siakudumisa")

Leader: Sing praises!
(Masithi!)

Group: Amen, we praise
  your name, O God!
(Amen, siakudumisa!)

Leader: Sing praises!
(Masithi!)

Group: Amen, we praise
  your name, O God!
(Amen, siakudumisa!)

Amen, amen.
(Amen, bawo.)

Amen, amen.
(Amen, bawo.)

Amen, we praise your
  name, O God!
(Amen, siakudumisa!)

Leader: Sing praises!
(Masithi!)

—South African traditional

The tune for this song can be found in *Songs for LiFE* (110, music by S. C. Molefe). If you don't have access to this music, use the words as a responsive reading. (Since these words are not copyrighted, you are free to make copies for your group.) Try the words in the South African tongue to remind yourselves that God's people around the world seek God's will and praise the King of kings.

Modeling the Character of Christ

Build Community
3 minutes

"Character," said evangelist Dwight Moody, "is what you are in the dark" (Ralph T. Mattson, *Visions of Grandeur*). Your individual character and the character of your working group will influence your effectiveness. Quickly compile a list of character traits you believe are important for good leadership. Write the list on an overhead transparency, chalkboard, or flipchart under the title "Character Traits of Leaders."

Open God's Word
2 minutes

Jesus' disciples were ordinary men of integrity. Their influence was profound. The story in Acts 4 suggests why this is so. In this passage, Peter and John have just healed a crippled man and are preaching to a crowd . . .

The priests and the captain of the temple guard and the Sadducees came up to Peter and John while they were speaking to the people. They were greatly disturbed because the apostles were teaching the people and proclaiming in Jesus the resurrection of the dead. They seized Peter and John, and . . . put them in jail.

The next day . . . they had Peter and John brought before them and began to question them: "By what power or what name did you do this?"

Then Peter, filled with the Holy Spirit, said to them: " . . . It is by the name of Jesus Christ of Nazareth, whom you crucified but whom God raised from the dead, that this man stands before you healed. He is 'the stone you builders rejected, which has become the capstone.'

"Salvation is found in no one else, for there is no other name under heaven given to men by which we must be saved."

When they saw the courage of Peter and John and realized that they were unschooled, ordinary

men, they were astonished and they took note that these men had been with Jesus.
—Acts 4:1-3, 5, 7-13

Reflect on the Word
2 minutes

Consider this quote from Ralph Waldo Emerson: "Every great institution is the lengthened shadow of a single man [woman]. His [her] character determines the character of the organization" (John Maxwell, *Developing the Leader Within You,* p. 35).

The disciples had been with Jesus. His character determined their character. His presence through the Holy Spirit enabled them to become bold, courageous men of integrity.

You have also been with Jesus; his character determines your character, the character of your group, and that of your congregation. Will anyone "take note that you have been with Jesus?" Encourage each member to reflect on this question personally.

Live Out the Word
10 minutes

If you had lived in Palestine when Jesus was ministering to the crowds, what character traits would have drawn you to follow Jesus? Share your answer with the group, and compile a list on an overhead transparency, chalkboard, or flipchart under the heading "Character Traits of Jesus."

Compare the first list you compiled on the traits of good leaders with this second list, and discuss these questions:

- What traits in the leader's list may run contrary to the person of Jesus? Would you like to add to or delete from either of the lists?
- How does your group's character as a whole measure up to your description of Jesus? Will people who deal with your group be able to say, "They have been with Jesus"?

Pray Together
3 minutes

Ahead of time, photocopy the prayer of commitment on page 74. Use the words of St. Francis of Assisi as a closing prayer. If you wish to sing this prayer, treat the last four lines as the refrain.

"Make Me a Channel of Your Peace"

All: *Make me a channel of your peace.*
Leader: *Where there is hatred, let me bring your love;*
where there is injury, your pardon, Lord:
and where there's doubt, true faith in you.

All: *Make me a channel of your peace.*
Leader: *Where there's despair in life, let me bring hope;*
where there is darkness, let me bring your light;
and where there's sadness, ever joy.

All: *Make me a channel of your peace.*
Leader: *It is in pardoning that we are pardoned;*
in giving to all people, we receive;
and in dying that we're born to eternal life.

All: *Master, grant that I may never seek*
so much to be consoled as to console,
to be understood as to understand,
to be loved as to love with all my soul.

—Francis of Assisi, 13th century

Creating Positive Change

Build Community
2 minutes

Life—congregational life included—is full of change. Talk about a time you resisted change. Why did you resist it? Do you believe you did the right thing? (Have group members share their answers with one or two others.)

Open God's Word
2 minutes

Change was guaranteed when Jesus arrived on the scene. In his Sermon on the Mount, Jesus says over and over, "You have heard it said . . . but I say . . . " Note how Jesus uses these words in reference to murder (vv. 21-22), adultery (vv. 27-28), divorce (vv. 31-32), oaths (vv. 33-34), an eye for an eye (vv. 38-39), and finally to love for enemies

(vv. 43-44). In this last reference, Jesus says:

"You have heard that it was said, 'Love your neighbor and hate your enemy.' But I tell you: Love your enemies and pray for those who persecute you, that you may be sons of your Father in heaven. He causes his sun to rise on the evil and the good, and sends rain on the righteous and the unrighteous. If you love those who love you, what reward will you get? Are not even the tax collectors doing that? And if you greet only your brothers, what are you doing more than others? Do not even pagans do that? Be perfect, therefore, as your heavenly Father is perfect."
—Matthew 5:43-48

Reflect on the Word
2 minutes

Jesus was challenging his Jewish listeners to change their viewpoint, to enlarge their understanding of how to live in a way that pleases God. Jesus challenges us to change as well. Jesus has a vision of who and what we will become as a new creation in him. But we can't become that new creation unless we change. This applies not only to individuals but also to the body of Christ. Jesus says, "Be perfect!" If we haven't arrived at perfection, it means we still need to grow and change.

Change is a scary word. It means leaving all that is familiar and adapting to what is new. It means giving up the security of knowing how things work and taking a risk to find a new way of looking at life. It means learning new behaviors and attitudes, growing, renouncing, and stretching. It may mean pain as we say goodbye to comfortable habits and beliefs that just don't conform to Christ's image. No wonder the body of Christ so often resists change.

Introducing change is not easy. But as a working group with leadership responsibilities, you are called to challenge others to grow, to become all that Christ wants us to be. You are called to be agents of change.

Live Out the Word
10 minutes

In his book *Teaching to Change Lives* (p. 45), Howard Hendricks throws this challenge out to every potential leader:

How have you changed . . . lately? In the last week, let's say? Or the last month? The last year? Can you be very specific? Or must your answer be incredibly vague? You say you're growing. Okay . . . how? "Well," you say, "in all kinds of ways." Great! Name one. You see, effective teaching [and leading] comes only through a changed person. The more you change, the more you become an instrument of change in the lives of others. If you want to become a change agent, you also must change.

Hendricks challenges each of us to evaluate our commitment to change and growth. How have we changed or grown physically, emotionally, spiritually, mentally, or socially? Use one or more of the exercises below to respond to the challenge. (Note that the first two deal with personal change; the second with group change. You may want to choose one of the personal options and then do the group option.)

Self-Assessment

Respond in writing by giving a very specific example of some way you have changed or grown in the past year. What circumstances led to the change, and how has it affected you? Now consider ways you personally wish to grow or change in the next year. Commit your desires to paper, and keep this "wish list" in your Bible.

Group Accountability

Together or in small groups of two or three, specifically describe to each other how you have grown or changed in the past year. What impact have these changes had on you, your work, your family, and your church? Describe areas in your life where you feel that you still need to grow and learn, and ask group members to hold you accountable.

Change Agent Evaluation

Evaluate your working group's role as an agent of change in light of Hendricks's assertion that "effective teaching [and leading] comes only through a changed person. The more you change, the more you become an instrument of change in the lives of others. If you want to become a change agent, you also must change." What change is your group trying to bring about in your church? How effective is your group in moving your congregation toward this change? How could your group become a more effective agent of change?

Pray Together
3 minutes

Close your devotional time by singing "Spirit of the Living God" (p. 54) or by praying the following prayer of commitment. After each statement, pause for a few seconds of silence so that group members can reflect on it and make it their own.

Lord God,
You have asked us to be perfect,
*   just as you are perfect.*
We confess that we need forgive-
*   ness every day for falling short*
*   of the mark.*
We thank you for clothing us with
*   righteousness   through   the*
*   blood of your son, Jesus Christ.*
Help us to strive for the high
*   calling you have placed on us*
*   because we are your children.*
Kindle in us, O Lord, a desire and
*   a willingness to be transformed*
*   through the Holy Spirit,*
to be your workmanship,
to shed those habits and desires
*   that dishonor your name,*
to be receptive to your cleansing
*   and refining*
to grow in the fruit of the Spirit.
We commit ourselves to you, O
*   Lord, wholly and completely.*
*   Amen.*

Called to Lead
Devotion Nine

Setting Goals

Build Community
3 minutes

Some people will do any-thing to get into the *Guinness Book of Records*. Their goal is to gain some kind of fame. What would you be willing to do to gain this kind of recognition? Why?

Open God's Word
1 minute

Our decisions and our actions reflect our goals. We find advice for goal-setting in these words from the book of Proverbs (photocopy this passage for group members or provide Bibles for everyone):

The plans of the mind belong to mortals,
but the answer of the tongue is from the LORD.
All one's ways may be pure in one's own eyes,
but the LORD weighs the spirit.
Commit your work to the LORD, and your plans will be established.
The LORD has made everything for its purpose,
even the wicked for the day of trouble.
All those who are arrogant are an abomination to the LORD;
be assured, they will not go unpunished.
By loyalty and faithfulness iniquity is atoned for,
and by the fear of the LORD one avoids evil.
When the ways of people please the LORD,
he causes even their enemies to be at peace with them.
Better is a little with righteousness
than large income with injustice.
The human mind plans the way,
but the LORD directs the steps.
—Proverbs 16:1-9,
New Revised Standard Version

Reflect on the Word
2-3 minutes

The Bible contains many stories of goal-setters whose goals were more worthy than achieving fame. Zacchaeus climbed a tree because he wanted to see Jesus. The ten lepers risked showing up in public because they wanted to

78

be healed by Jesus. Queen Esther, braving death, confronted the king to save her people from destruction. The apostle Paul endured beatings, stoning, shipwreck and more because he wanted to spread the gospel. (If you have time, think of others who made it into God's book of records. Hebrews 11 names a number of these faith heroes.)

Working groups in the church also need to set goals to guide their actions. Goals are directional signs for nearly all that we do. They help us establish priorities, sort out choices, plan our work, and motivate us to achieve results. Without goals, our work may be ineffective and unsatisfying. In the words of baseball great Yogi Berra, "If you don't know where you are going, you'll probably end up someplace else."

The apostle Paul put a more spiritual spin on goal-setting. "I press on toward the goal to win the prize for which God has called me heavenward in Christ Jesus." In the end, the ultimate goal for all that we do is to bring glory to God.

Live Out the Word
10-11 minutes

Perhaps your working group was given a set of goals, or maybe you're in the process of defining or refining your goals. Regardless of where you are in the process, the two exercises suggested here can help you clarify where you are going.

Biblical Principles

What principles for goal-setting and decision making do you find in the Scripture passage from Proverbs? (Look for clues in these key words: plans, motives, commit, works, proud, love and faithfulness, fear, pleasing ways, righteousness, course, steps.) Write the principles on a transparency, chalkboard, or flip chart.

Group Goals

In pairs, write (on a transparency or flip chart) three goals for your group's work this season that reflect these principles. Briefly share the goals with the larger group, and tell why you think these goals are important at this time for your group's ministry. Give your written statements to your group's chairperson for further discussion at a later time. (If you have time now, arrive at a group consensus as to which goals should guide your work.)

Pray Together
3 minutes

Spend some time in prayer with your working partners, thanking God for past guidance and petitioning God for

79

future guidance. Pray for each other's personal needs so that you can function effectively as a team member in achieving God's goals for your group.

Close your time together once again with the song "Lead Me, Guide Me" (p. 57) or with this song:

"Lord, Be Glorified"

In our lives, Lord, be glorified, be glorified,
in our lives, Lord, be glorified today.

In our homes . . .
In your church . . .
In your world . . .

Devotion Ten

Open to Others

Build Community
3 minutes

All of us live and work with others. As group members think quietly about this fact, have each write down the heading "People are . . . " on a sheet of paper. Then invite them to complete the sentence by writing down as many positive or negative attributes as come to mind in the next minute or so. Ask them to share the one that best reflects their interactions with people on this particular day.

Open God's Word
2 minutes

The gospels are full of stories about Jesus' encounters with people—usually crowds of them, as we see in this story:

During those days another large crowd gathered. Since they had nothing to eat, Jesus called his disciples to him and said, "I have compassion for these people; they have already been with me three days and have nothing to eat. If I send them home hungry, they will collapse on the way, because some of them have come a long distance."

His disciples answered, "But where in this remote place can anyone get enough bread to feed them?"

"How many loaves do you have?" Jesus asked.

"Seven," they replied.

He told the crowd to sit down on the ground. When he had taken the seven loaves and given thanks, he broke them and gave them to his disciples to set before the people, and they did so. They had a few small fish as well; he gave thanks for them also and told the disciples to distribute them. The people ate and were satisfied. Afterward the disciples picked up seven basketfuls of broken pieces that were left over. About four thousand men were present. And having sent them away, he got into the boat with his disciples and went to the region of Dalmanutha.

The Pharisees came and began to question Jesus. To test him, they asked him for a sign from heaven. He sighed deeply and said, "Why does this generation ask for a miraculous sign? I tell you the truth, no sign will be given to it." Then he left them, got back into the boat and crossed to the other side.

—Mark 8:1-13

Reflect on the Word
3 minutes

As a member of a working group or ministry team, you cannot avoid working with people. Neither could Jesus and his disciples.

People came to listen to Jesus and stayed for three days. Perhaps the disciples were thinking, "What reckless, irresponsible behavior. Don't these people realize that they should plan ahead or else go home when the food runs out?" But Jesus didn't see careless people; he saw sheep without a shepherd, more hungry for spiritual truth than earthly sustenance. And he responded to both needs.

Jesus could have said, "Well, if I can spend forty days in the wilderness without food, this crowd can surely survive till they get home." Instead, Jesus fed them by means of a miracle. Can you imagine how that miracle affected them? Because Jesus was open to people's needs, everyone received a blessing.

Jesus didn't just cater to people, though. The Pharisees, who wanted to test Jesus by asking for their own personal miraculous sign, got a cold shoulder. Jesus responded with a deep sigh and a firm answer.

When we are called to lead, we are also called to respect and to be open to the people we are leading. That's not always easy. Being open to people means that their needs will influence you; in fact, their needs may come before your agenda. Being open to people means that you value their gifts and contributions and take them seriously. Being open to people means you will be vulnerable to exploitation.

But that's what's required. In *Community That Is Christian: A Handbook on Small Groups* (p. 262), Gorman writes: "To lead means to affect and also to be affected by those who follow. It involves influencing and being influenced, initiating and responding, being giver and receiver." Jesus put it even more simply: "But you are not to be called 'Rabbi,' for you have only one Master and you are all brothers. . . . For whoever exalts himself will be humbled, and whoever humbles himself will be exalted" (Matt. 23:8, 12).

Live Out the Word
8 minutes

What's your "PQ" (People Quotient)? When you completed the sentence "People are . . . ," how many attributes were positive and how many were negative? On a transparency, chalkboard, or flipchart, list them under the headings "Positive" and "Negative." Using the scale below, how would you rate your group's assessment of people *in general?*

- Overwhelmingly negative— You're candidates for the Grinch Hall of Fame.
- Somewhat negative—You're candidates for the Yes, But . . . Club.
- Neutral—You're members of the Bland Pudding Fancier's Society.
- Somewhat positive—You're candidates for Cheerleaders' Grad School.
- Overwhelmingly positive— You're graduates of Pollyanna Tech.

Now take another look at the list of positive and negative attributes. Which ones describe the people you've been called to serve? (Circle these words on the list.) Use the scale again to determine your "PQ" with this *specific* group of people. What does this rating say about your group's openness to the people you serve? Be honest in your evaluation. Praise God if your rating leans toward the positive; seek God's guidance for ways to move in that direction if your rating leans toward the negative.

Pray Together
4 minutes

Many people received a blessing because Jesus was open to people. Perhaps you too have been blessed when you opened yourself to other people and reached out to meet a need. Share some of these moments with each other.

Close your session with a prayer of thanksgiving for the many ways people can enrich each other's lives. Pray for open ears, eyes, and hearts to be effective in your ministry. Or sing or read the words of this song as your closing prayer:

"O Master, Let Me Walk with Thee"

O Master, let me walk with thee
  in lowly paths of service free;
tell me thy secret; help me bear
  the strain of toil, the fret of care.

Help me the slow of heart to
  move by some clear, winning
  word of love;
teach me the wayward feet to
  stay, and guide them in the
  homeward way.

83

*Teach me thy patience; still with
thee in closer, dearer company,
in work that keeps faith sweet
and strong, in trust that
triumphs over wrong.*

*In hope that sends a shining ray
far down the future's
broadening way,
in peace that only thou canst
give, with thee, O Master, let
me live.*

—Washington Gladden, 1879

Devotion Eleven

The *Same* Attitude

Build Community
3 minutes

In her book *Sportin' a 'Tude: What Your Attitude Says When You're Not Looking*, Patsy Clairmont says, "Attitudes. We don't really enjoy talking about them (unless they're someone else's). For when we do, they're seldom positive, often offensive, and just like colds—very easy to catch."

Have your group share one attitude they've "sported" in the last day or two that was contagious. How did their attitudes positively or negatively affect others around them?

Open God's Word
2 minutes

The apostle Peter tells us to keep our attitudes heavenly minded while doing earthly good. He writes:

Therefore, since Christ suffered in his body, arm yourselves also with the same attitude, because he who has suffered in his body is done with sin. As a result, he does not live the rest of his earthly life for evil human desires, but rather for the will of God.

The end of all things is near. Therefore, be clear minded and self-controlled so that you can pray. Above all, love each other deeply, because love covers over a multitude of sins. Offer hospitality to one another without grumbling. Each one should use whatever gift he has received to serve others, faithfully administering God's grace in its various forms. If anyone speaks, he should do it as one speaking the very words of God. If anyone serves, he should do it with the strength God provides, so that in all things God may be praised through Jesus Christ. To him be the glory and the power forever and ever. Amen.

—1 Peter 4:1-2, 7-11

Reflect on the Word
3 minutes

As a working group you are called to lead *and* to help others—to provide support, make decisions, cast a vision, and give advice, among other

85

things. You are called to serve and to be a servant. That doesn't sound very glamorous or even very rewarding. At some point you've probably heard someone who works in a task group within the church remark, "It's a thankless job, but somebody has to do it."

The apostle Peter knows about serving others. He travels from place to place helping churches organize themselves, guiding them in decision making, casting vision, and giving advice. As thanks for all of that, he gets to live out of a suitcase, often far away from home and family, and even gets thrown in jail from time to time. It's a thankless job.

But Peter doesn't bemoan his lot in life. When he thinks of all that Christ suffered, Peter can hardly complain. Others might observe his life and see sacrifice and suffering; Peter rejoices because his service to the church brings glory to God.

We are called to serve. Our mandate is to use whatever gift God has given us with all our strength and to do it with the same attitude as Christ had when he freely gave his life for us. In Peter's words, we are to be self-controlled, clear-minded, hospitable, loving, cheerful, and gracious.

Inasmuch as we do that for Christ, we bring honor, and praise, and glory to the name of Christ, who gave everything for us. It's as simple—and as rewarding—as that.

Live Out the Word
10 minutes

Allow time for group members to assess their own attitude about serving in your working small group. (You'll want to make a photocopy of the exercise on p. 88 for each group member.)

If you have time, share the results of the first two parts of this survey with one or two others in your group. As a whole group, brainstorm ways for overcoming negative attitudes about serving in your working group. Use the last part of the exercise to help you determine which tasks best fit each member of your group.

Pray Together

Follow up the self-assessment exercise with a recommitment to godly service. Lead with these prayer prompts and allow time for silent prayer or go around the circle and give people a chance to respond with short prayers.

Dear Lord, I admit that when I examine my heart and spirit, I find that my attitude is less than perfect. In particular, I confess that I feel negative about . . .

Lord, I pray that you will change my attitude to be in line with yours. In love, you gave everything so that we could have a new life. Help me also to be filled with your love and to offer myself gladly, without grumbling. In Jesus' name. Amen.

Conclude your time together by singing this familiar spiritual:

"Lord, I Want to Be a Christian"

Lord, I want to be a Christian in my heart, in my heart.
Lord, I want to be a Christian in my heart.

In my heart, in my heart,
Lord I want to be a Christian in my heart.

Lord, I want to be more loving . . .

Lord, I want to be more holy . . .

Lord, I want to be like Jesus . . .

—Afro-American spiritual

How's *My* Attitude?

Peter tells us to arm ourselves with a Christ-like attitude and to serve in a way that brings praise to God. Check your own attitude about serving in this working group by completing the three exercises below.

Circle the attitude that best describes how you feel about serving in this working group.

Serving in this working small group is . . .

- a chore (but someone has to do it).
- a bore (so many tedious details).
- a door (to learning new things and meeting new people).
- more (I love it, gimme more of this stuff!).

Circle the reason that best describes why you find yourself serving in this working small group.

I'm involved in this ministry because . . .

- I wanted to get out of the house/office/school.
- volunteer work teaches me new skills and increases my marketability.
- I like the people involved and wanted to be with them.
- my skills and gifts intersect with this ministry's goals.
- somebody twisted my arm; I felt duty-bound to help out.
- other (add your own reasons).

Rate your attitude towards these tasks that working group members are frequently expected to do.

(5 indicates a very positive attitude, 1 indicates a very negative attitude)

5 4 3 2 1   Deciding (thinking about and discussing issues clearly)

5 4 3 2 1   Reasoning (making objective rather than emotional decisions)

5 4 3 2 1   Praying (listening for God's leading rather than following my own ideas)

5 4 3 2 1   Loving (extending myself for someone else's benefit)

5 4 3 2 1   Offering hospitality (helping others feel comfortable and welcomed)

5 4 3 2 1   Administering (organizing for effective ministry)

5 4 3 2 1   Communicating (getting out the written or spoken message)

5 4 3 2 1   Serving (using my gifts and resources for another person's benefit)

5 4 3 2 1   Other (add any other tasks that are specific to your group)

Devotion Twelve

Bringing Hope

Build Community
2 minutes

Talk to each other about a time when something that seemed almost hopeless became a reality. (If your group is large, divide into smaller groups of two or three people.)

Open God's Word
1 minute

Jeremiah was a prophet who offered hope to the people of Israel in their captivity. He delivered this message from God:

This is what the LORD says: "When seventy years are completed for Babylon, I will come to you and fulfill my gracious promise to bring you back to this place. For I know the plans I have for you," declares the LORD, "plans to prosper you and not to harm you, plans to give you hope and a future. Then you will call upon me and come and pray to me, and I will listen to you. You will seek me and find me when you seek me with all your heart. I will be found by you," declares the LORD, "and will bring you back from captivity. I will gather you from all the nations and places where I have banished you," declares the LORD, "and will bring you back to the place from which I carried you into exile."
—Jeremiah 29:10-14

Reflect on the Word
3 minutes

Life without hope—can there be anything worse? That's where the exiled Israelites found themselves. This is the condition today of a world and a society that doesn't know God. Things are bad, and it seems as though they will never get better.

Then, into the void comes a voice of hope, inspired by God's love and Spirit. There is a way out of the pit after all, and sunbeams appear over the horizon. This is the precious gift that Jeremiah delivered to Israel and the gift God's people can offer to a hurting world.

God's gift of hope motivates us to serve. The pastor preaches, the choir sings, the teacher guides, the counselor counsels, the youth leaders lead, the ushers greet, working group members meet in the hope that their actions will meet needs.

And in acting, we are offering God's gift of hope to hurting, confused people. We can offer a vision of a future that includes forgiveness and a new life with God. Words and deeds expressing hope through Christ are a tremendous gift we can give to those who come to us in our work. "Hope deferred makes the heart sick, but a longing fulfilled is a tree of life" (Prov. 13:12). Our gift of hope restores life to people, and they in turn will bear fruit.

If hope is the ointment that salves a troubled heart, then God's love through his Holy Spirit is the bottle that holds the ointment. We cannot offer our own hope; it would run out. But God's Spirit of hope never runs out, never disappoints. It is a privilege to have been anointed by that hope, and a greater privilege to be able to offer it to others.

Live Out the Word
10 minutes

Have your group imagine that Jeremiah has been hired as a consultant to help your congregation work through things that seem to be hindering your working group and others in the church from accomplishing your calling. (Provide photocopies of the "A Consultation with Jeremiah" exercise (p. 91) and Bibles for each group member.)

Pray Together
4 minutes

It's your privilege and responsibility to offer hope to those you serve. You are not working alone—God is the source of your hope, and so you can pass a message of hope on to others. This song based on Isaiah 40:31 can help your group reflect on this hope:

"Those Who Wait upon the Lord"
Those who wait upon the Lord
*   shall renew their strength,*
they shall mount up on wings as
*   eagles;*
they shall run and not be weary,
*   they shall walk and not faint.*
Help us, Lord; help us, Lord, in
*   your way.*

Those who love the God of life . . .

Those who live a life of love . . .

—Stuart Hamblen. © 1953, Hamblen Music Co., 26101 Ravenhill Rd., Canyon Country, CA 91350. Used by permission.

Spend time praying together for the needs in your church that your working group can address and listening for messages of hope you can deliver.

End your time of prayer with this benediction that Paul wrote to the Romans (bless each other by reciting it in unison as you lay your hand on the shoulder of the person sitting or standing on your right):

May the God of hope fill you with all joy and peace as you trust in him, so that you may overflow with hope by the power of the Holy Spirit.
—Romans 15:13

A Consultation with Jeremiah

What's the major problem or challenge facing your congregation? If Jeremiah were to come to your congregation, which "pit of hopelessness" might he find?

- the black hole of financial distress
- the cesspool of hidden sin
- the dump of unforgiven hurts and pain
- the wasteland of broken relationships
- the dry desert of "Why bother?"
- the maze of confusion and indecisiveness
- the swamp of unfulfilled potential
- or [add your own descriptions of hopelessness that your church might be facing]

What message of hope from God might Jeremiah offer your congregation?

As a group, try to pinpoint the diagnosis and prescription Jeremiah might give about the challenges your congregation is experiencing. Especially consider how Jeremiah's advice could impact the work your group is called to do. Build each other up in the Lord.

Devotion Thirteen

Others First

Build Community
2 minutes

Sometimes we give lip service to the goal of putting others first. Have group members think about the numerous tasks that need doing around the house. Is there a menial job that they refuse to do or almost never volunteer to do? What is it, and why do they refuse to do it?

Open God's Word
1 minute

The message of the apostle Peter is "Do whatever needs doing!" Although Peter addresses this passage to elders, it applies to other leaders too.

To the elders among you, I appeal as a fellow elder, a witness of Christ's sufferings and one who also will share in the glory to be revealed: Be shepherds of God's flock that is under your care, serving as overseers—not because you must, but because you are willing, as God wants you to be; not greedy for money, but eager to serve; not lording it over those entrusted to you, but being examples to the flock. And when the Chief Shepherd appears, you will receive the crown of glory that will never fade away. . . . In the same way be submissive to those who are older. All of you, clothe yourselves with humility toward one another, because "God opposes the proud but gives grace to the humble." Humble yourselves, therefore, under God's mighty hand, that he may lift you up in due time. Cast all your anxiety on him because he cares for you.
—1 Peter 5:1-7

Reflect on the Word
6 minutes

There are no little people in God's kingdom.

The people of Jesus' day may have questioned that statement. Teachers of the law and rulers, they believed, were most worthy of respect and awe and sat up on the top rungs of the leadership ladder. Far down below sat the little people: the women and children, the tax collectors, the lepers and Samaritans. (Encourage group members to honestly think about the "ladder" in your church. Are some people at the bottom?)

But Jesus turned that ladder upside down. "So the last will be first, and the first will be last," he said (Matt. 20:16). And just in case his disciples didn't get it, Jesus demonstrated the principle. Tying a towel around his waist, he knelt before his followers and washed their dusty feet (John 13:1-17). He called a little child to stand among his disciples and said, "Whoever humbles himself like this child is the greatest in the kingdom of heaven" (Matt. 18:3). The gospel writers tell us that Jesus dined with a despised tax collector, healed lepers and blind people, and offered living water to a woman of ethnic minority and dubious character.

Your task group must exercise its leadership humbly, "not lording it over" others but eager and willing to serve. In his book *Paths of Leadership* (p. 29), Andrew Le Peau says:

A leader, a servant, is someone who can identify the hurts, the concerns, the areas needing growth or strengthening in others and who then pours in healing and nourishment. . . . If we have caught God's priority for people, for whole people, we will look for all these needs.

Identify some of the hurts and concerns members of your congregation experience, particularly focusing on those your working group can address.

Mahatma Gandhi sometimes left his public campaigns for India's independence and went back to the little village where he grew up. He would sit at a spinning wheel and spin thread to experience more clearly the lives of the people for whom he struggled. Great causes, he realized, should never elevate us above simple duties. If Gandhi, who never claimed to be a Christian, could show such a Christ-like spirit, can we do less?

Live Out the Word
6 minutes

Peter's charge to Christian leaders to put others first involves both attitudes and tasks. He urges leaders to be eager to serve, to be examples to the flock, to be obedient, to serve as overseers, to avoid greed, to be submissive to older people, and to humble themselves.

In small groups of two or three, discuss these questions:

• Does the call to put others first mean you have to put

yourself and your own needs second?

- What, for you, is the most difficult part about this call to serve, particularly in this working group?

Have a person in each group record the specific difficulties that are raised (write each issue on a separate index card). For example, someone in your group might say, "I find it hard to seek out other people's ideas when I already have so little time to serve," or, "When people complain about the work our group does, I get very discouraged."

Quickly identify difficulties that were raised by more than one person in your group, and suggest a possible way to alleviate the problem. Is time available for service a major issue for your group? (Maybe you need to add another person or two to your committee to lighten the load.) Or is discouragement a major concern? (Consider asking members of the congregation to serve as prayer partners.)

Pray Together

5 minutes

Peter knows how difficult it is sometimes to serve others, but he also knows about the blessings we experience by obeying God's call: "You will receive the crown of glory that never fades away" (v. 4). He charges us to humble ourselves "under God's mighty hand, that he may lift you up in due time. Cast all your anxiety on him because he cares for you" (vv. 6-7).

During this prayer time, praise God for the opportunity to serve. (You may want to go around the circle and give everyone a chance to offer a sentence of humble gratitude.) Then distribute the cards to those who volunteer to pray for the specific anxieties you've listed. Use the notes as guidelines for your prayers, committing these feelings, thoughts, and issues to God's care. Close by singing this song to each other:

"The Servant Song"

Will you let me be your servant,
*   let me be as Christ to you?*
Pray that I might have the grace
*   to let you be my servant too.*

—Richard Gillard. © 1977, Scripture in Song (a division of Integrity Music, 1000 Cody Rd., Mobile, AL 36695). All rights reserved. Used by permission.

Loving as Jesus Loves

Build Community
3 minutes

We are "dearly loved children" of God. (Eph. 5:1). Picture the loving arms of our heavenly Father wrapped around each group member as you ask this question: If you were to sing a love song to Jesus, what song would you choose? (You may want to sing one or two now or later on during your closing prayer time.)

Open God's Word
1 minute

Be kind and compassionate to one another, forgiving each other, just as in Christ God forgave you. Be imitators of God, therefore, as dearly loved children and live a life of love, just as Christ loved us and gave himself up for us as a fragrant offering and sacrifice to God.

For you were once darkness, but now you are light in the Lord. Live as children of the light, (for the fruit of the light consists in all goodness, righteousness and truth) and find out what pleases the Lord.
  —Ephesians 4:32; 5:1-2, 8-10

Reflect on the Word
1 minute

The Bible could be called a love letter from God to his people, and the image of love that you get when you read the Bible is one of sacrifice, of giving, and of offering up oneself just as Christ did for his beloved children.

Romantic love is sweet and pretty; God's love is tough and gritty. It is not pretty to give up one's life for others. Yet God asks his servants to be imitators of him. God is asking you for tough love, the kind of love that hangs in there when the sweetness is gone. The world needs to see love in action.

When you find that you do not have it in you any more to give that kind of love, take this verse to heart. Remember that you are a dearly loved child of God, who gave his life for you. The wonder of it takes your breath away. Embrace his love, and rejoice in it. Reflect on

God's mercy in your life, and ask God to supply your need. A God who gave you so much will also give you the grit you need to keep loving when it seems that there's nothing left inside you to give.

Live Out the Word
10 minutes

At a church leadership conference at the Crystal Cathedral, Pastor Juan Carlos Ortiz told church leaders about the shortest sermon he ever preached. It was this: "Love one another." After preaching it, he sat down. There were other sermons he wanted to preach to his congregation, he told them, but until they actually put this most basic of lessons into practice, there was no point in preaching anything else.

Ortiz was illustrating a very fundamental principle: we must master the first step in a discipline before we can move on to the second step. The foundation must be strong before we can build on it.

"Love one another!" Together or in small groups, discuss the implications of this message for your work using the following questions to guide you:

- What does this three-word sentence mean to you?
- In what concrete ways can you show love for others in your group?
- In what specific ways can your group show love to the people you serve?

Encourage group members to commit to carrying out a concrete expression of love for each other and for those they serve. Ask them to choose an accountability partner to whom they'll report and who will support them in their commitment to do this before the next meeting.

Pray Together
5 minutes

Spend time during this meeting praising God for redeeming you, calling you, and sustaining you. Invite group members to choose songs from your own hymnal or songbook that are personal favorites and to tell why this particular song means so much. Sing some of these or the "love songs" members chose earlier.

Then commit your "love one another" promises to God with this prayer:

Dear Lord, you've heard our expressed desires to love one another more. You know how easy it is for us to forget our good intentions when we leave this meeting, so we commit our promises to you.

96

We implore you to listen to our hearts as we silently offer ourselves to be models of your self-sacrificing love. Hear us, we pray, in Jesus' name, Amen.

You may wish to begin and/ or end your prayer by singing this refrain:

"Jesu, Jesu, Fill Us with Your Love"
Jesu, Jesu, fill us with your love, show us how to serve the neighbors we have from you.

—Folk song from Ghana, adapted by Tom Colvin. © 1969, Hope Publishing Company, 380 S. Main Pl., Carol Stream, IL 60188. All rights reserved. Used by permission.

Modeling Faith, Hope, and Love

Build Community
3 minutes

In an old country gospel tune a mother tells her son, "Remember, son, live your faith every day, for you may be the only Good Book people will read today."

Is there a person in your life who has modeled faith, hope, and love in such a way that you've been influenced to follow Christ? Describe that person to a partner.

Open God's Word
2 minutes

We continually remember before our God and Father your work produced by faith, your labor prompted by love, and your endurance inspired by hope in the Lord Jesus Christ.

For we know, brothers [and sisters] loved by God, that he has chosen you, because our gospel came to you not simply with words, but also with power, with the Holy Spirit and with deep conviction. You know how we lived among you for your sake. You became imitators of us and of the Lord; in spite of severe suffering, you welcomed the message with the joy given by the Holy Spirit. And so you became a model to all the believers in Macedonia and Achaia. The Lord's message rang out from you, not only in Macedonia and Achaia—your faith in God has become known everywhere.

—1 Thessalonians 1:3-8

Remember your leaders, who spoke the word of God to you. Consider the outcome of their way of life and imitate their faith.

—Hebrews 13:7

Reflect on the Word
2 minutes

Faith is more caught than taught. This cliche contains a kernel of truth. When people see a life of real faith in action, they use that life as a model for their own faith journey.

Paul and the Thessalonians are examples of that. First Paul

98

came to them, living a sacrificial life and preaching the message of salvation. The Thessalonians saw and beieved; they modeled their lives on Paul's life. But his influence didn't stop there—the Macedonians and Achaians were inspired by the Thessalonians and praised God as well for their faithful lives. In fact, the Thessalonians were models of faith, hope, and love for people everywhere.

This has serious, almost scary implications for kingdom workers. People are watching us, reading us like a book to see if what we do matches what we say and believe. Hidden in Paul's words of thanksgiving is the key to defusing that fear. Almost as an afterthought, to the phrase "you became imitators of us" he adds the words "and of the Lord" (v. 6). As leaders and workers, we will indeed be models of faith, hope, and love, but it is because of the work of the Holy Spirit that we can be imitators of Christ, the perfect model.

Paul is not saying that we must model perfection; rather, he is saying that our work must reflect the faith, hope, and love we experience in Jesus. This is not of our own making, but a gift worked in us with joy from the Holy Spirit. Pass it on!

Live Out the Word
8 minutes

Review the items on your agenda with your group before doing the discussion exercise below. Point out the agenda items that will need decisions, the steps that will require making plans for the future, the issues that may demand more information. Emphasize that as you deal with each of these items you will be working by faith, inspired by hope, and prompted by love. Discuss how your working group can model faith, hope, and love in word and deed. Think of specific ways you can carry out your work so that others in your congregation will see Jesus in you and welcome the message of the gospel with joy. Ask a volunteer to write down the ideas on newsprint or the chalkboard so that they are in front of you as you proceed with the meeting.

Pray Together

Say a prayer of commitment using the prayer of St. Francis introduced in devotion 7 (p. 74) or the prayer on the next page.

*Our Father, we pray that
we may model the good news
of Jesus Christ not "simply
with words, but also with
power, with the Holy Spirit
and with deep conviction."
We pray for your power to
flow through us and for the
courage to live out our faith
in the tasks you have given
us to do. Amen.*

Conclude the time of commitment by singing one or more of the following songs (or others from the list of songs on pp. 145-146 in the back of this book).

- "Spirit of the Living God" (words on p. 54)
- "Lead Me, Guide Me" (words on p. 57)
- "O Master, Let me Walk with Thee" (words on p. 57)

Devotion Sixteen

Seeing the Best in Others

Build Community

2 minutes

Our names are part of our identity. Have each group member tell what his or her name means. (You may want to bring a book that lists names and their meanings. Check your local library, bookstore, or doctor's office, or ask new parents in your congregation if they have a book.) Then ask each one to consider this question: Have you lived up to your name?

Or ask group members to list common Bible names and what they mean. (Have Bibles available for research.) Did these Bible characters live up to their names?

Open God's Word

3 minutes

Barnabas, Paul's coworker, was aptly named. He's first mentioned in Acts in connection with the early church.

Joseph, a Levite from Cyprus, whom the apostles called Barnabas (which means Son of Encouragement), sold a field he owned and brought the money and put it at the apostles' feet.
—Acts 4:36

Next, we meet Barnabas after Saul's conversion.

When [Saul] came to Jerusalem, he tried to join the disciples, but they were all afraid of him, not believing that he really was a disciple. But Barnabas took him and brought him to the apostles. He told them how Saul on his journey had seen the Lord and that the Lord had spoken to him, and how in Damascus he had preached fearlessly in the name of Jesus. So Saul stayed with them. . . .
—Acts 9:26-28

When news of a great Christian awakening in Antioch reached Jerusalem, the disciples sent Barnabas to check it out.

When he arrived and saw the evidence of the grace of God, he

101

was glad and encouraged them all to remain true to the Lord with all their hearts. He was a good man, full of the Holy Spirit and faith, and a great number of people were brought to the Lord.

—Acts 11:23-24

Even though John Mark had deserted Paul and Silas (Acts 13:13), it was Barnabas who took the risk and parted company with Paul in order to give John Mark another chance to serve.

Barnabas wanted to take John, also called Mark, with them, but Paul did not think it wise to take him, because he had deserted them in Pamphylia and had not continued with them in the work. They had such a sharp disagreement that they parted company. Barnabas took Mark and sailed for Cyrus. . . .

—Acts 15:37-39

Reflect on the Word
3 minutes

Barnabas and his nephew Mark were Paul's companions on his first missionary journey. Unfortunately, young Mark bailed out quite quickly and returned to Jerusalem. Barnabas and Paul carried on their mission very successfully, visiting and preaching the gospel to many towns in Asia Minor.

Put yourself in Barnabas's place for a moment, and imagine that it was your nephew who had deserted an important ministry. How would you greet this young man when you met him again face to face? Would you give him the cold shoulder? Make a sarcastic remark? Berate him, lecture him, see if he's learned his lesson? (Allow time for the group to think about what their first response might be.)

Scripture doesn't record exactly what Barnabas said, but we can read between the lines. When Paul said, "Barnabas, let's see how the new church plants are coming along," Barnabas said, "Yes, let's go, and let's take Mark along." That idea resulted in a "sharp disagreement" between Paul and Barnabas. They parted company, with Paul taking Silas as his new partner and Barnabas taking Mark. Mark got a second chance.

Barnabas truly lived up to the name Son of Encouragement. He saw real potential in Mark, and Mark became a faithful servant. Although Mark is not mentioned in the rest of Acts, Peter and Paul both mention him warmly in their later epistles, speaking of his helpfulness and care (1 Peter 5:13; Col. 4:10; 2 Tim. 4:11). It may have been this same Mark who forever left his stamp on Christianity with the gospel he wrote about his loving, forgiving Savior, Jesus Christ.

Sometimes we're tempted to write people off because of past mistakes, or we make negative assumptions about them because they've disappointed us. Thankfully, God doesn't do that with his children; think of Matthew, the tax collector, Peter, who denied Christ, Paul, the self-righteous Pharisee, you and me. The God of second chances sees the best in people. Regardless of our names, we can encourage others to serve God.

Live Out the Word
8 minutes

We could call Paul, Barnabas, and Mark a "working group" called to ministry by the church at Jerusalem. Think back about your team and the work your group has been doing as you discuss these questions:

• Which one of the three characters in this story do you most identify with: Mark the quitter, Paul the cautious one, or Barnabas the encourager? (Be honest with each other, and recognize that at some point you've probably felt like each of these team members.)

• Has your group experienced a similar situation? (Perhaps someone you were counting on let you down, or you needed to go back to your starting point, or you're considering splitting into two teams.)

• What encouragement can you take from the end result of this story? (God is at work! Identify specific ways group members are sensing this right now.)

Pray Together
3 minutes

Invite your group to spend time *listening* to God, rather than talking to God. For the next few moments, individually ask the Lord to reveal how you can practice the good news of God's gracious second chance in thought, word, and deed. If a thought occurs to you, or if the Lord is gently nudging you in regard to your relationships with others, write down these insights as a reminder to act on these ideas. (Make sure that each person has a pencil and paper available.)

At the close of the silent prayer time, join in singing or reading the words of the song on the next page as a prayer.

"God, You Call Us To This Place"

God, you call us to this place,
*   where we know your love and*
*   grace.*
Here your hospitality makes of us
*   one family,*
makes our rich diversity richer
*   still in unity,*
makes our many voices one,
*   joined in praise with Christ*
*   your Son.*

Now assembled in Christ's name,
*   all your mercies to proclaim—*
in the hearing of your word, in
*   our prayer through Christ the*
*   Lord,*
in the ministries we share,
*   learning how to serve with*
*   care—*
in the Spirit let us be one in faith
*   and unity.*

In the water we were born of the
*   Spirit in the Son.*
Now a priestly, royal race rich in
*   every gift of grace—*
called, forgiven, loved, and freed,
*   for the world we intercede:*
gather into unity all the human
*   family.*

—Delores Dufner, OSB.
© 1993, OCP Publications,
5536 NE Hassalo,
Portland, OR 97213.
Used by permission.

Devotion Seventeen

Working Behind the Scenes

Build Community
3 minutes

Few of us find ourselves in the spotlight. And most of us appreciate the people who work behind the scenes, even though we often fail to say so. Encourage group members to describe unsung heroes in their lives, someone who affected them positively. Then covenant together to thank these people in the next week with a note, a phone call, a small gift, or a visit.

Open God's Word
1 minute

In his final greetings to the Colossians, Paul mentions a number of fellow workers. Except for Mark, Barnabas, and Luke, we read very little about these people in Scripture. Note Paul's appreciative words.

Tychicus will tell you all the news about me. He is a dear brother, a faithful minister and fellow servant in the Lord. I am sending him to you for the express purpose that you may know about our circumstances and that he may encourage your hearts. He is coming with Onesimus, our faithful and dear brother, who is one of you. They will tell you everything that is happening here.

My fellow prisoner Aristarchus sends you greetings, as does Mark, the cousin of Barnabas. (You have received instructions about him; if he comes to you, welcome him.) Jesus, who is called Justus, also sends greetings. These are the only Jews among my fellow workers for the kingdom of God, and they have proved a comfort to me. Epaphras, who is one of you and a servant of Christ Jesus, sends greetings. He is always wrestling in prayer for you, that you may stand firm in all the will of God, mature and fully assured. I vouch for him that he is working hard for you and for those at Laodicea and Hierapolis. Our dear friend Luke, the doctor, and Demas send greetings.

—Colossians 4:7-14

Reflect on the Word
4 minutes

Without people working behind the scenes, very little would happen in this world. We may never see the workers behind the carton of milk, the Internet technology, the space shuttle launch, or the miracles of modern medicine.

It's the same in the church. Scratch beneath the surface of a program, a worship service, a church social, an outreach ministry and you'll find the unsung heroes who are responsible. (Take a minute or two to name some of these servants in your church family. Think of ways you might let them know they're appreciated.)

While most Christians today know something about Paul's story—the places he visited, the people who found the Lord through his ministry, the perils he encountered—probably only biblical scholars are familiar with the names of the people who worked to make it happen. Someone had to be the scribe, arrange the boat tickets, carry the messages, and generally facilitate Paul's ministry, but these people's names are known only as footnotes in the Bible, afterthoughts tacked on to the end of Paul's letters. In the letter to the Colossians, you'll find a doctor, a prayer warrior, a messenger, an encourager, and a comforter, for starters. They're all identified as servants for the Lord.

You too are called to serve your congregation, perhaps behind the scenes. It's quite possible you won't get thanks, recognition, honor, or even have your work acknowledged. You are the Epaphras, the Tychicus, the Justus of this world. But you will grow in the grace of the Lord Jesus Christ, because grace is the byproduct of service.

Live Out the Word
8 minutes

When we look at an iceberg floating in the ocean, we can only see about one-tenth or less of its total mass. The rest is beneath the water.

Make a visual representation of the work for which your group is responsible by drawing an iceberg on an overhead or on the chalkboard. Draw the waterline on the iceberg. Above the line, write all those aspects of your work that are visible or known to the congregation. Underneath the line, write the invisible or behind-the-scenes jobs.

Consider how effective the ministry of your group would be if you neglected those aspects of your work that are behind the scenes. Honestly discuss with each other your feelings about this aspect of your work. Do you sometimes resent the fact that nobody appreciates or recognizes this contribution to the well-being of the church? How can you deal with these feelings?

Pray Together
4 minutes

Thank God for the work entrusted to you by ending this session with singing and prayer. Let the words of this old hymn serve as a prayer:

"Take My Life That It May Be"
Take my life that it may be all
you purpose, Lord, for me.
Take my moments and my days;
let them sing your endless
praise.

Take my hands and let them
move at the impulse of your
love.
Take my feet and lead their way;
never let them go astray.

Take my voice and let me sing
always, only for my King.
Take my lips and keep them true,
filled with messages from you.

Take my motives and my will,
all your purpose to fulfill.
Take my heart—it is your own; it
shall be your royal throne.

Take my love; my Lord, I pour at
your feet its treasure store.
Take myself, and I will be yours
for all eternity.

—Frances R. Havergal, 1874;
rev. *Psalter Hymnal,*
CRC Publications, 1987.

Follow your song by asking each member of your group to pray specifically for one of the tasks that you listed below the line on the iceberg drawing. Encourage group members to pray about this part of your work in the coming weeks.

Devotion Eighteen

A Humble Spirit

Build Community
2 minutes

"Most of us know we'll never be the greatest," says Richard Foster in *Celebration of Discipline* (p. 126). "Just don't let us be the least."

Oswald Chambers puts it another way: "Humble yourself—it is a humbling business to knock at God's door—you have to knock with the crucified thief" (*Treasures from My Utmost for His Highest*).

Ponder these two quotes for a minute and then ask group members these questions: Are Foster and Chambers saying the same thing? Which one most closely reflects your own humility?

Open God's Word
2 minutes

A humble spirit is essential if we are to serve others, says Paul.

If you have any encouragement from being united with Christ, if *any comfort from his love, if any fellowship with the Spirit, if any tenderness and compassion, then make my joy complete by being like-minded, having the same love, being one in spirit and purpose. Do nothing out of selfish ambition or vain conceit, but in humility consider others better than yourselves. Each of you should look not only to your own interests, but also to the interests of others.*

Your attitude should be the same as that of Christ Jesus: Who, being in very nature God, did not consider equality with God something to be grasped, but made himself nothing, taking the very nature of a servant, being made in human likeness. And being found in appearance as a man, he humbled himself and became obedient to death—even death on a cross!

—Philippians 2:1-8

Reflect on the Word
2 minutes

When we think about a humble spirit, we suddenly have many questions: It's great to be humble . . . but how low do you go? There's a limit, isn't there? Isn't there something ironic about trying to be humble? The harder you try, the more you can be proud of your humility. What a paradox it is that the greatest Christians are often the most humble!

These questions and thoughts show just how hard it is for self-centered humans—even redeemed self-centered humans—to be humble saints. It's a puzzle to many people.

Humility comes from the Latin word *humus,* meaning fertile soil. We don't usually think much about soil; it's just there under our feet all the time. And yet, when seeds drop into it, the soil gives nourishment, and the seed is able to take root and grow. In fact, the more fertilizer that's been put into the soil in the form of manure, compost, and decaying vegetation, the stronger and healthier is the plant that grows in it.

So perhaps the secret of humility is this: our souls are like the soil, and enriching our souls with the fertilizer of prayer and praise, Scripture and meditation, and the fellowship of godly friends and counselors will produce healthy fruit. When we earnestly seek these disciplines, we forget about ourselves and focus on God instead. And that's the beginning of true humility.

Then, as Paul suggests, we'll "do nothing out of selfish ambition or vain conceit, but in humility consider others better than [ourselves]" (v. 3). We'll look not only to our own interests, but also to the interests of others. Our attitude will be molded into that of Christ Jesus, who even though he was God, thought nothing of taking on human form and emptying himself for our salvation.

That's an awesome, truly humbling thought!

Live Out the Word
10 minutes

The spirit is nourished and grows in Christ-like character by practicing spiritual discipline. Traditionally, twelve spiritual disciplines have been identified. "The purpose of the disciplines," writes Foster in *Celebration of Discipline* (p. 2), "is liberation from the stifling slavery to self-interest and fear."

Invite your group to take a look at the role spiritual disciplines can play in developing an attitude of humility. (Make a photocopy of the twelve disciplines and the four questions on p. 110 for each group member.)

Spiritual Disciplines and Humility

In groups of two or three, describe how one or more of the twelve spiritual disciplines listed below have helped you grow spiritually.

Inward Disciplines:
• Meditation
• Prayer
• Fasting
• Study

Outward Disciplines:
• Simplicity
• Solitude
• Submission
• Service

Corporate Disciplines:
• Confession
• Worship
• Guidance
• Celebration

Discuss these questions:
• Which of the disciplines has especially helped you to develop a spirit of humility?
• What do you find most difficult about cultivating a humble spirit?
• Which disciplines could help you grow in this area? How?
• What holds you back from exploring these disciplines?

Pray Together

Close your time together by praying for each others' needs as they've been shared in your small group. Then sing this song based on the two verses that follow the passage from Philippians 2 selected for this devotion:

"He Is Lord"

He is Lord, he is Lord,
he is risen from the dead, and he
*   is Lord!*
Every knee shall bow, every
*   tongue confess*
that Jesus Christ is Lord.

He is King, he is King,
he will draw all nations to him;
*   he is King!*
And the time shall be when the
*   world shall sing*
that Jesus Christ is King.

He is Love, he is Love,
he has shown us by his life that
*   he is Love!*
All his people sing with one voice
*   of joy*
that Jesus Christ is Love.

He is Life, he is Life,
he has died to set us free, and he
*   is Life!*
And he calls us all to live
*   evermore,*
for Jesus Christ is Life.

—Anonymous, based on
Philippians 2:10-11; John 12:32

Devotion Nineteen

Common Courtesy

Build Community
2 minutes

Parents constantly tell their children, "Mind your manners." Have group members tell what manners they learned as a child that are absolutely ingrained into their character today. Who taught them this? Which particular circumstances or events made this lesson stick?

Open God's Word
3 minutes

We don't need a book on etiquette to remind us how to treat each other. We can find such advice in the Bible. For example, consider Paul's words to Titus:

Remind the people to be subject to rulers and authorities, to be obedient, to be ready to do whatever is good, to slander no one, to be peaceable and considerate, and to show true humility toward all men.

At one time we too were foolish, disobedient, deceived and enslaved by all kinds of passions and pleasures. We lived in malice and envy, being hated and hating one another. But when the kindness and love of God our Savior appeared, he saved us, not because of righteous things we had done, but because of his mercy. He saved us through the washing of rebirth and renewal by the Holy Spirit, whom he poured out on us generously through Jesus Christ our Savior, so that, having been justified by his grace, we might become heirs having the hope of eternal life.

—Titus 3:1-7

Reflect on the Word
2 minutes

Common courtesy doesn't have a very good reputation these days. The practice of following social rules for behavior has been called artificial, trivial, hypocritical, elitist, stuffy, and more. Who needs etiquette and manners, anyway?

The Bible, however, seems to place a high value on common courtesy. Paul tells Titus, "Be

111

peaceable and considerate" (v. 2). In the New Century Version, this verse is translated, "Be gentle and polite to all people." James tells readers that "the wisdom that comes from above is first of all pure; then peace-loving, considerate, submissive, full of mercy and good fruit, impartial and sincere" (James 3:17). Peter says, "Live as servants of God; show proper respect to everyone" (1 Pet. 2:16-17).

Courtesy is sometimes called the grease that oils the wheels of social interaction. But it's more than that. When we treat someone with courtesy, we are acknowledging the value of that person and affirming their worth. Sometimes little acts of courtesy can speak loudly. When we ask people how they're doing, thank them for their work, treat them with dignity, respect their privacy, apologize when we've made a mistake, and never chastise them publicly, we are giving them a message that says, "We honor you as an imagebearer of God."

Missionaries understand how important it is to understand the rituals of a social culture. Without this understanding, and without respect for other people's practices, they wouldn't be able to get a hearing for the gospel. It's the same in our own culture—when we treat people with respect, we'll be received and heard.

Live Out the Word
8 minutes

You've heard these sayings many times:

If you can't say something nice, don't say anything at all.
Say you're sorry.
Don't take the biggest piece.

Your group probably uncovered many more of these social rules with the community-building exercise.

How can you translate some of these common rules of courtesy into specific actions for your working group? Have group members work together in pairs or as a whole group to come up with your own list of "top ten" ways to treat people with courtesy. These should be workable principles that you can use as guidelines to carry out your group's tasks. For instance, practice "Always say thank you" by sending a note or making a phone call to everyone who volunteers time and gifts to your group's ministry. You may want to assign members to each of these ten practices.

Pray Together
4 minutes

Use the ACTS formula—Adoration, Confession, Thanksgiving, Supplication—for your prayer time. Introduce each step with a short sentence prayer followed by a time of silence so that members can add their own prayers.

Adoration: *Lord God, you have created everything in this world, and you created us. You made us to be imagebearers of your greatness. O God, you are so great.*

Confession: *Lord, we confess that often we have not always treated others as though they were your image-bearers. We pray for forgiveness.*

Thanksgiving: *We thank you, Father God, that you valued us so much that you gave your Son Jesus Christ to die for our sins. We offer our hearts and our lives to you in thanksgiving.*

Supplication: *We pray, Holy Spirit, that you will inspire us to see others as God's creation, worthy of respect and consideration. We pray for humble, serving hearts to bring your message of grace and love.*

Conclude your time together by joining hands and singing the refrain of "Jesu, Jesu" (p. 97) or this chorus:

"This Is My Commandment"
This is my commandment that
*   you love one another,*
that your joy may be full.
This is my commandment that
*   you love one another,*
that your joy may be full.
That your joy may be full,
that your joy may be full.
This is my commandment that
*   you love one another,*
that your joy may be full.

—Anonymous

113

A Community of Diversity

Build Community
4 minutes

Your working small group is a TEAM. As you write these four letters on a transparency, chalkboard, or flipchart, point out that there's no "I" in "team." Working in groups of two or three, discuss and write a definition of "team." Combine these statements into one working definition that best describes the kind of team you want your working group to be.

Open God's Word
1 minute

The church at Antioch was unique. Today we might call it a "pilot project," since it was the first Gentile church established outside Judea and the mother of all the rest. The Bible tells about its leadership team and how it operated.

In the church at Antioch, there were prophets and teachers: Barnabas, Simeon called Niger, Lucius of Cyrene, Manaen (who had been brought up with Herod the tetrarch), and Saul. While they were worshiping the Lord and fasting, the Holy Spirit said, "Set apart for me Barnabas and Saul for the work to which I have called them." So after they had fasted and prayed, they placed their hands on them and sent them off.

—Acts 13:1-3

Reflect on the Word
3 minutes

It's hard to imagine a more diverse team than the one that led the church at Antioch:

- Barnabas. A Levite and Jew from Cyprus, he was a recognized leader in the early church who had sold land and donated the money to the apostles.
- Simeon. His name suggests a Jewish background; also called "Niger," which may refer to a dark complexion.
- Lucius of Cyrene. Lucius is a Latin name, and Cyrene was

the capital of Libya in Africa. He may have been a freed slave.

- Manaen. A Hebrew, he was the foster brother of the hated Herod Antipas.
- Saul. A Roman citizen steeped in Greek culture and Hebrew religion, he was a new convert whose zealous persecution of Christians was transformed into a passion for spreading the gospel.

What turned a group of individuals with different gifts and agendas into a unified working group that God used powerfully? The story in Acts gives a simple prescription: they spent time together with God. They all worshiped and fasted, they all listened to the Holy Spirit, and they all prayed. And when it was time to send off a ministry team, they all gave their blessing and support. They were able to arrive at decisions because God was the leader of their team.

The leadership team at Antioch Church is a great model for an effective working group ministry team. This community of diversity

- was unified because Christ was at its center.
- placed a priority on seeking God's will.
- blessed others with its gifts.

Live Out the Word
8 minutes

Perhaps your working group has been together for some time, or you may just be getting started. Either way, spend time discovering the diversity of backgrounds and ideas within your group. Choose one or two of the following activities depending on the size of your group and the time available.

Thumbnail Sketches

Our working group is also a diverse community. Each person is unique because of our different geographic, family, and spiritual backgrounds. How would the writer of Acts describe each member of our ministry team? Give a thirty-second, one-sentence thumbnail sketch of yourself, including your geographic, ethnic, and spiritual background.

Sentence Starters

Often we work side by side without really recognizing what team members bring to the team or how they feel about being part of a team. To help us get a better picture of each other, complete these sentences:

- The strength (or gift) I can bring to this group is . . .

- The thing I enjoy most about working in a small group is . . .

Give participants time to complete each sentence in writing before sharing it with the group. You'll receive a greater variety of answers and more honesty if they have time to reflect before hearing what others have to say.

Pictured Principles
For this exercise, cut out pictures of groups (a crowd at a sports event, a class of school children, a rock group, and so on) from magazines or newspapers. Give each member (or pairs) one picture and these directions:

Groups operate in different ways to accomplish purposes. Study the picture you've been given, and find a positive principle about group interaction that could apply to our group. For instance, a sports team illustrates the principle that team members rely on each others' strengths to get the job done.

Pray Together
4 minutes
Sing a worship song such as "Father, We Adore You," "Hear Our Prayer, O Lord," or "Spirit of the Living God" (p. 54) to move your group into a prayerful spirit. Join hands to form a prayer circle as you sing.

The leadership community at Antioch worshiped, prayed, fasted, and listened before they made any decisions. Based on that model, lead in prayer or ask for volunteers to pray that your group will develop

- a spirit that adores God by . . .
- a spirit of prayer for . . .
- a spirit that denies itself and seeks God's will for . . .
- a listening spirit open to the Holy Spirit's leading regarding . . .

Devotion Twenty-One

I'll Pray for You

Build Community
3 minutes

Invite group members to imagine themselves in this situation:

Two friends of yours, members of your working group, feel called to street ministry. They spread the gospel through mime presentations in downtown parks and often attract crowds. During one of their forays into the inner city, they're warned by police to stop their work because they're violating a city ordinance. What would you say to your friends?

- Just stay cool until the heat's off, then start up again.
- They can't do that! We'll write letters of protest to city hall.
- If it's against the law, you should quit. Christians must obey the authorities.

- Maybe this is God's way of saying that this isn't your ministry.
- [Your own response].

Did your group come up with a variety of responses, or did they generally agree on one response?

Open God's Word
2 minutes

Shortly after the Holy Spirit came to them at Pentecost, Peter and John were taken before the Sanhedrin to explain why they were preaching in public. The court charged them to quit preaching about Jesus. Then Peter and John were set free.

On their release, Peter and John went back to their own people and reported all that the chief priests and elders had said to them. When they heard this, they raised their voices together in prayer to God. "Sovereign Lord," they said, "you made the heaven and the earth and the sea and everything in them. You spoke by the Holy Spirit through the mouth of your servant, our father David: 'Why do the nations rage and the peoples plot in vain? The kings of the earth take their stand and the rulers gather together against the Lord and against his Anointed One.' Indeed Herod and Pontius Pilate met together with the Gentiles and the people of Israel in this city to conspire against your holy servant Jesus, whom you anointed. They did what your power and will had decided beforehand should happen. Now, Lord, consider their threats and enable your servants to speak your word with great boldness. Stretch out your hand to heal and perform miraculous signs and wonders through the name of your holy servant Jesus."

After they prayed, the place where they were meeting was shaken. And they were all filled with the Holy Spirit and spoke the word of God boldly.

—Acts 4:23-31

Reflect on the Word
2 minutes

A number of phrases in this Scripture passage stand out:
- "Peter and John went back to their own people. . . . " As soon as they were set free, Peter and John looked for support from people who loved them. Peter and John needed other people.
- "They raised their voices together in prayer." Prayer wasn't a matter of asking God to bless their decisions;

prayer *was* the decision they made. Prayer was first, last, and in between.
- "Now Lord, consider . . . enable . . . stretch out your hand . . . perform . . ." They didn't ask God, "Now what do we do?" Peter and John and their support group seemed to know the answer to that question: they were to stay true to their calling. But because they had a problem, they asked God to act. And God did! Immediately, the place was filled with the Holy Spirit, and they spoke the word of God boldly. How's that for an answer to prayer?

Live Out the Word
4 minutes

Your group has a calling, a specific task to accomplish for your church. Do members of your congregation know about your calling? Do they know your needs? Discuss together how you can "go back to your own people" to encourage them to be your prayer support team.

Notice again the action verbs the prayer warriors in the early church used to petition God to act. Then brainstorm a list of action words that describe what you want God to do through your group to accomplish your calling. (Write them on a transparency, chalkboard, or flipchart.) Raise your voices, saying these words together as a prayer of petition.

Pray Together
9 minutes

As a community called together, your working small group can be a tremendous support for each member, just as the early followers of Christ were for Peter and John. Your prayers of intercession can make you co-laborers with the Lord in accomplishing his work through others.

Divide the group into prayer partners. Encourage partners to share needs and concerns about their work and their personal lives and to identify specific kinds of support they need from your working group. (Allow three to four minutes for this sharing time; provide notecards and pencils for recording prayer requests.)

Then invite your group to spend a brief time in silence to attune yourselves to God before praying. "We begin to pray for others by first quieting our fleshly activity and listening to the quiet thunder of the Lord of Hosts" (Foster, *Celebration of Discipline*, p. 39).

When you sense the group feels quieted, invite partners to pray for each other's needs. Pray in the full expectation that God is eager to hear and answer. (Allow four to five minutes for prayer.)

If you have time, conclude your prayer time by singing "Hear, Our Prayer O Lord," "Lord, Listen to Your Children Praying" (p. 57), or sing this song from Zimbabwe:

"If You Believe and I Believe"
*If you believe and I believe, and
we together pray,
the Holy Spirit will come down
and set God's people free,
and set God's people free, and set
God's people free;
the Holy Spirit will come down
and set God's people free.*

—from Zimbabwe,
based on Matthew 18:19

Music for this song can be found in *Songs for LiFE* (242, CRC Publications). If you don't have the music, consider using just the words. Ask the group to join in on the phrase "and set God's people free."

Where's Your Heart?

Build Community
3 minutes

We all need encouragement to carry on for the Lord, but what about admonition? Take an honest look at your working group. If the apostle Paul were part of this group, what admonishment—or encouragement—might he offer? (Provide two different colors of notecards and have group members write one admonishing and one encouraging statement on each.) Collect these for use later in the session.

Open God's Word
2 minutes

Paul and Peter were both apostles in the early church. Paul's ministry was to the Gentiles, while Peter's was mainly to the Jewish community. The early days of the Christian church were explorations into uncharted territory. The leaders had to make decisions about doctrine and policies, especially when it came to following Jewish laws about food and circumcision. Not everyone saw matters in the same way, and meetings weren't always harmonious. Here's how Paul describes one of them:

When Peter came to Antioch, I opposed him to his face, because he was clearly in the wrong. Before certain men came from James, he used to eat with the Gentiles. But when they arrived, he began to draw back and separate himself from the Gentiles because he was afraid of those who belonged to the circumcision group. The other Jews joined him in his hypocrisy, so that by their hypocrisy even Barnabas was led astray.

When I saw that they were not acting in line with the truth of the gospel, I said to Peter in front of them all, "You are a Jew, yet you live like a Gentile and not like a Jew. How is it, then, that you force Gentiles to follow Jewish customs?

"We who are Jews by birth and not 'Gentile sinners' know that a man is not justified by observing the law, but by faith in Jesus

Christ. So we, too, have put our faith in Christ Jesus that we may be justified by faith in Christ and not by observing the law, because by observing the law no one will be justified."

—Galatians 2:11-16

Reflect on the Word
2 minutes

The dictionary defines accountability as "an obligation or willingness to accept responsibility or to account for one's actions." Accountability isn't a very popular concept these days. It's uncomfortable in a society that places a high value on tolerance for other peoples' beliefs. It's time-consuming too, especially with all the other responsibilities that weigh on us. Mostly we'd rather live and let live.

But imagine how church history might have changed if Paul had not held Peter accountable for his behavior. When Peter visited the new church at Antioch, he felt free to eat Gentile food with the Gentile believers. But when some Jewish Christians arrived from Jerusalem, Peter refused to eat with the Gentiles for fear of what the Jewish Christians might think. Paul realized that the principle of "justification by faith" was at stake; this issue was too important for him to keep silent.

Your working group is a community of believers. That means you are accountable to each other. You are accountable for accomplishing the tasks this group has set out to do, and you are also accountable to each other for living out your faith every day. This group can be a place where you ask each other, "Where's your heart?" Asking that question can be uncomfortable and time-consuming as you deal with the answers. But as this Scripture passage shows, it's also rewarding and can make a big difference in God's kingdom.

Live Out the Word
10 minutes

Set aside the notes of encouragement for the time being. To strengthen the spirit of accountability in your group, answer one or both of these questions:

- *Does the shoe fit?* Read aloud the admonishments written at the beginning of this session, encouraging people to comment on or clarify each one. Decide as a group whether the admonishment does apply to your group and whether action should be taken. (If your group is large, divide into smaller groups, letting each group deal with a portion of the written responses. Allow

121

time to share with the larger group.)

- *Do we practice accountability?* Quickly read through the admonishments collected at the beginning of the session as an acknowledgement that there is room to grow within your group. Discuss how members of this group hold each other accountable for their Christian walk and for completing their tasks. Then consider what techniques might be helpful for increasing accountability in your group. Here are some ideas:

  - Choose accountability partners to call or meet each other on a regular, predetermined basis.
  - Choose someone with the gift of encouragement to call people to make sure they're completing assigned tasks and to offer encouragement.
  - Have a "spiritual check-in" as part of the agenda during which people know they can share and talk openly about problems.
  - Choose a person from outside this group to conduct a quarterly pastoral visit to the group and ask evaluative questions.
  - Set aside one meeting quarterly to evaluate both

the work and the spiritual growth of the group.

You may want to choose one or more members to write up an accountability plan and a concrete proposal for implementing your ideas.

Pray Together
4 minutes

As a prelude to your prayer time, read the notes of encouragement that were also written. End your session with a prayer of praise, confession, petition, and thanks. Invite members to participate, using these suggested prayer prompts.

Dear Lord, we praise you for your unconditional love in choosing us to follow you. We praise you for . . .

We know that we fall short of the mark in completing our work. We confess . . .

We rely on your strength and guidance. We pray especially for . . .

We see your goodness to us. We thank you Lord for . . .

Amen.

Close your time together by singing "Lord, Be Glorified" (p. 80).

Devotion Twenty-Three

How Are You Feeling?

Build Community
3 minutes

Color can set a mood or describe how we're feeling. Invite group members to select a crayon from a box of crayons (bring a large box so that you have several shades of the basic colors) that best describes how they're feeling about their day. Have each member explain why they selected that particular color. Give a clue or two if needed, but let group members give their own creative reasons. (Perhaps you selected blue because you feel at peace—or a bit down—about your day. Maybe someone selected gray to reflect a "blah" day, yellow to describe a cheerful feeling, green to describe a growing day, red a vibrant—or embarrassing— feeling.) Have members write their names on the colors chosen, and collect them in a basket for later in the session.

Open God's Word
3 minutes

The Bible tells many stories about times when people wore their feelings on their sleeves. Here are some examples:

When Pharaoh's horses, chariots and horsemen went into the sea, the LORD brought the waters of the sea back over them, but the Israelites walked through the sea on dry ground. Then Miriam the prophetess, Aaron's sister, took a tambourine in her hand, and all the women followed her, with tambourines and dancing. Miriam sang to them. . . .

—Exodus 15:19-21

So Moses went down to the people [camped at the foot of Mount Sinai] and told them. And God spoke all these words: "[the Ten Commandments]. . . ."
When the people saw the thunder and lightning and heard the trumpet and saw the mountain in smoke, they trembled with fear.

—Exodus 19:25; 20:1-18

My soul is in anguish. . . . I am worn out from groaning; all night long I flood my bed with weeping and drench my couch with tears.
—Psalm 6:3, 6

Jezebel sent a messenger to Elijah to say, "May the gods deal with me, be it ever so severely, if by this time tomorrow I do not make your life like that of one of them."

Elijah was afraid and ran for his life. . . . He came to a broom tree, sat down under it and prayed that he might die. "I have had enough, LORD," he said. "Take my life; I am no better than my ancestors."
—1 Kings 19:2-4

Even today my complaint is bitter; his hand is heavy in spite of my groaning.
—Job. 23:2

In the fourteenth year of King Hezekiah's reign, Sennacherib king of Assyria attacked all the fortified cities of Judah and captured them. Then the king of Assyria sent his field commander. . . .

The commander stood and called out . . . "Who of all the gods of these countries has been able to save his land from me? How then can the LORD deliver Jerusalem from my hand?"

When King Hezekiah heard this, he tore his clothes and put on sackcloth and went into the temple of the LORD.
—Isaiah 36:1-2, 13, 20; 37:1

Reflect on the Word
2 minutes

God is a God of feelings: "You, O Lord, are a compassionate and gracious God, slow to anger, abounding in love and faithfulness" (Ps. 86:15). Feelings are God's gift to his children and reflect God's image in them.

Without feelings, we'd be mere robots, moving through life like automatons. There would be no songs of joy like Miriam's, no standing in awe before the presence of God like the children of Israel, no expression of agonizing pain like David's, no admission of despair like Elijah's, no outlet for bitterness like Job's, no mourning like Hezekiah's.

But we do have feelings, and they color our world every day. Positive feelings lift us up; feelings of depression, anger, fear, and weariness pull us down into the pit. Our feelings affect our personal and family life as they did for David and Job, our communal life as they did for Miriam and the children of Israel, and our leadership roles as they did for Elijah and Hezekiah.

Live Out the Word
8 minutes

Have your group make a list of words used in the Bible to describe feelings. (The *NIV Study Bible* is a handy reference. You'll find words like anger, anxiety, cry, love, dismay, fear, hate, and many more.) List these words on a transparency, chalkboard, or flipchart.

What do we do with these feelings? We may want to hide or deny some of them because they don't seem to fit into the Christian life. But saints like Elijah and David expressed their feelings openly, with healing results. We can too!

Your working group is a Christian community where you should be able to speak openly and honestly about your feelings. The various gifts in a community of believers—discernment, encouragement, knowledge, and teaching, for instance—can bring healing and hope. The community is strengthened when you share joys and sorrows. The community is a gift from God so that you will know you are not alone.

To encourage openness in your group, spend a minute or so establishing ground rules such as these:

- Only share as you are comfortable.
- Feel free to pass when it's your turn.
- All feelings and thoughts shared are confidential and will never be repeated outside the group.
- Members will treat each other with respect and consideration.

Using the colors chosen earlier as a starting point, invite group members to share their feelings briefly with the group. Why is a group member feeling blue (at peace or down) today? Continue around the circle until everyone who wishes to share has had an opportunity to express his or her feelings, explain what has brought on the feelings, and ask for prayers of thanksgiving or petition.

Pray Together
4 minutes

Bring out the basket of crayons with names written on them and have everyone draw a crayon, making sure they don't pick their own. Spend time in silent prayer, with each person praying for the person whose name they've drawn. Send the crayons home to remind group members to pray at least once in the next week for the person whose name they've drawn. (Bring the crayons back, and draw again next week if you want to continue this exercise.)

Conclude your time together by singing or reflecting quietly on these words:

"Those Who Wait upon the Lord"

*Those who wait upon the Lord
  shall renew their strength,
they shall mount up on wings as
  eagles;
they shall run and not be weary,
  they shall walk and not faint.
Help us, Lord; help us, Lord, in
  your way.*

Those who love the God of life . . .

Those who live a life of love . . .

—Stuart Hamblen. ©1953, Hamblen Music Co., 26101 Ravenhill Rd., Canyon Country, CA 91350. Used by permission.

Devotion Twenty-Four

I Hear What You're Saying

Build Community
3 minutes

True friends are a gift from God. What makes them so precious? A good friend . . .

- has a sense of humor.
- has good communication skills.
- is a good listener.
- is loyal.
- has shared interests.

List these five characteristics on a transparency, chalkboard, or flipchart and invite your group members to participate in a survey. Ask them to rate the characteristics from one to five, with five being the most important. Total the ratings for each characteristic. Which one rated highest in your group? (A recent survey rated listening as the most important characteristic of a friend.)

Open God's Word
2 minutes

An old proverb says, "God gave us two ears and one mouth so that we could hear twice and speak once." The Bible also talks about the importance of listening. Here are some examples:

Do not be quick with your mouth, do not be hasty in your heart to utter anything before God. God is in heaven and you are on earth, so let your words be few. As a dream comes when there are many cares, so the speech of a fool when there are many words.
—Ecclesiastes 5:2-3

My dear brothers, take note of this: Everyone should be quick to listen, slow to speak and slow to become angry.
—James 1:19

He who answers before listening—that is his folly and his shame.
—Proverbs 18:13

Reflect on the Word
2 minutes

In *The Road Less Traveled* (pp. 120-121), Morgan Scott Peck says, "The principle form that the word of love takes is attention. When we love another, we give him or her our attention; we attend to that person's growth. . . . By far the most common and important way in which we can exercise our attention is by listening." Solomon and James echo this advice in Scripture. Listening in itself is a sacred gift that we can give to each other.

When you are called together in community, you will have many opportunities to listen to each other. That's not an easy task. Listening skills aren't often taught in classrooms or places of work, even though most people spend three times as much time listening as reading and five times as much time listening as writing.

When you listen to someone, you tell them that your attention is focused on their needs, that you are trying to understand them, that they are valuable enough for you to take time for them. Such a message of caring reflects the Spirit of God and points the way to Jesus.

Live Out the Word
10 minutes

Discuss together or in groups of two or three how you can help each other become better listeners. Focus on some or all of the following activities (and be sure to practice good listening skills while doing so!):

- The Chinese characters that depict the verb meaning "to listen" include the symbols for the ear, the eyes, the heart, and undivided attention. How do each of these contribute to good listening?
- Tell about a time when someone really listened to you, and describe what made the person a good listener. From these examples, make a list of the top ten signs that indicate you're talking to a good listener.
- Talk about your frustrations when you feel you weren't heard in a specific situation. How could the situation have been changed?
- Make a list of your top ten "poor listener" pet peeves. (For example, a listener yawns in the middle of your story.)

Pray Together
3 minutes

Thank God that even when we fail, God always listens to his children. Invite members of your group to suggest favorite songs about talking to God or choose "What a Friend We Have In Jesus" or "Lord, Listen to Your Children Praying" (p. 57).

Use these words as your closing prayer:

"O LORD, you have searched me and you know me. You know when I sit and when I rise; you perceive my thoughts from afar. You discern my going out and my lying down; you are familiar with all my ways. . . . Such knowledge is too wonderful for me" (Ps. 139:1-3, 6).

Thank you, God, that even before we say a word, you are listening. Send your Spirit to help us listen to others. Amen.

Devotion Twenty-Five

How May I Help You?

Build Community
3 minutes

Clip a variety of pictures from newspapers and magazines that show people together (playing, working, grieving, celebrating, and so on). Give one to each person in your group with these directions:

What does this picture suggest to you when you think about the question, Why do people need people? Write a sentence expressing your thoughts, and read your sentence aloud to the group.

Open God's Word
1 minute

God created people because he wanted to live in fellowship with us. We're created in God's image, and we too need to live in fellowship with God and with others. Listen to what the Bible says about people needing people:

The LORD God said, "It is not good for the man to be alone. I will make a helper suitable for him."

—Genesis 2:18

Two are better than one, because they have a good return for their work: if one falls down, his friend can help him up. But pity the man who falls and has no one to help him up! Also, if two lie down together, they will keep warm. But how can one keep warm alone? Though one may be overpowered, two can defend themselves. A cord of three strands is not quickly broken.

—Ecclesiastes 4:9-12

We who are strong ought to bear with the failings of the weak and not to please ourselves. Each of us should please his neighbor for his good, to build him up. For even Christ did not please himself but, as it is written: "The insults of those who insult you have fallen on me."

—Romans 15:1-3

Carry each other's burdens, and in this way you will fulfill the law of Christ.

—Galatians 6:2

Reflect on the Word

2 minutes

Almost every hero of faith had someone standing beside him or her to be a cheerleader, guide, supporter, coworker, and friend. Moses asked God for someone and got Aaron; Noah had his sons; Naomi and Ruth were a team, as were Esther and Mordecai; David loved Jonathan and later relied on Joab; Jesus called his disciples; Paul had Barnabas and Silas as mission partners, and his letters mention many other helpers.

People need people. People of God especially need each other. As a group of workers in God's kingdom, you too need each other for support, guidance, encouragement, friendship, prayer, and accountability. Carrying our burdens alone is not biblical.

Paul uses the Greek word *bear,* referring to the heavy load a soldier might carry on a trek, when he tells Galatians to carry each other's burdens. Imagine walking beside a friend who is staggering under a monstrous load while you stroll along unencumbered. But when you take part of the load, you can walk together at the same pace, sharing the burden and having fellowship.

Christ showed the way when he took our burden of sin upon himself. And now he calls us to bear each other's burdens. That's what people who live in Christian community do.

Live Out the Word

8-9 minutes

Supporting and caring for others can only happen when people reveal their burdens in a safe environment. Choose one of the following activities to explore the issues of disclosure (talking about your needs) and confidentiality (knowing that matters won't be repeated outside the group.) Your choice of activities will depend on how caring and close your group already is. You may want to work together or break into smaller groups of two or three.

Disclosure

Opening up to each other doesn't just happen. What would keep you from sharing your needs within this group? How can you become more supportive of each other?

Support

Make a list of the answers you wrote down in response to the question Why do people need people? Now evaluate your group in light of these answers. Is your group helping to meet these needs? What changes would make your group better able to support each other?

Sharing Burdens

What burdens are you carrying that you would like to share with others? (These may be needs related to your personal life or related to your work in this group.) Name a practical way that the group can help you carry this burden.

Confidentiality

What does confidentiality mean to you? If your group doesn't already have one, can you agree to a "covenant of confidentiality" that defines this term? How will you deal with a breach of confidentiality?

Pray Together
3-4 minutes

Your prayer time should reflect what has happened during this session. If people in the group shared hurts and burdens, you may want to bring these people into the center of a circle, lay hands on them, and pray for their needs. Or your group may be eager to spend extended prayer time praying for one another's needs. On the other hand, your group may still feel uncomfortable with disclosure, and your prayer time should respect those feelings. Pray for God's leading and blessing, and for his healing touch on the lives of your group members.

Sing "The Servant Song" (p. 94) to close your time together.

Devotion Twenty-Six

Together We're Strong

Build Community
4 minutes

Imagine that your group is stranded on an isolated island. Everyone needs to work together to survive and thrive. Based on what they've observed about people's abilities and gifts, have group members match up the following tasks with persons in your group (you may want to write the tasks on a transparency, chalkboard, or flipchart):

- head honcho: organizes everyone
- creative thinker: finds unique solutions for problems
- protector: nurtures people's emotional needs
- hands-on operator: does the nitty-gritty practical stuff
- spiritual guide: provides encouragement, points to God
- trouble-shooter: thinks ahead, pinpoints problems
- historian: connects past and future, records events
- comedian: tickles people's funny bones
- [name and describe other roles your group members might play in this situation]

Are you missing someone to fulfill one of the roles? What are your chances of survival without this person?

Open God's Word
2 minutes

Teamwork is God's idea. God created our physical bodies as a unit, and Paul uses this analogy to describe the body of Christ.

The body is a unit, though it is made up of many parts; and though all its parts are many, they form one body. So it is with Christ. For we were all baptized by one Spirit into one body— whether Jews or Greeks, slave or free—and we were all given the one Spirit to drink. Now the body is not made up of one part but of many. If the foot should say, "Because I am not a hand, I do not belong to the body," it would not for that reason cease to be part of the body. And if the ear should say, "Because I am not an eye, I do not belong to the body," it would not for that reason cease to be part of the body. If the whole body were an eye, where would the sense of hearing be? If the whole body were an ear, where would the sense of smell be? But in fact God has arranged the parts in the body, every one of them, just as he wanted them to be. If they were all one part, where would the body be? As it is, there are many parts, but one body.

—1 Corinthians 12:12-20

Reflect on the Word
1 minute

If Paul were writing to your working group instead of to the church in Corinth, perhaps his message could be paraphrased as follows:

Your working group is a unit; though it is made up of many members, the many members form one working group. So it is with Christ. For as believers, we form the body of Christ—whatever our ethnic background, profession, gender, IQ, income, talents—and God's Spirit equips us to do our tasks here. Now our group does not consist only of the strongest voice; it takes all of us to speak the truth. If the quiet person says, "Because I do not speak up, I'm not part of this group," he would not for that reason cease to be part of the body. And if the creative thinker should say, "Since I seem to be on a different wavelength, I don't belong here," she would not for that reason cease to be part of the body. If the whole group consisted of administrators, who would provide the word of wisdom? If the whole group consisted of teachers, who would provide the gifts of mercy and shepherding? But in fact God has arranged to bring many different gifts into this body, every one of them, just as God wanted them to be. If we were all the same, how could we accurately represent the many-splendored Christ to this world? As it is, there are many voices, many gifts, many strengths and weaknesses, but only one body. That's us.

Take a minute to appreciate the diversity of gender, ethnic origin, educational background, professional experience, and personality types represented in your group. Add your own thoughts to the paraphrased passage. Are you feeling like one body?

Live Out the Word
8 minutes

So what's your gift? Perhaps not everyone in your group has a ready answer to that question. We can discover our spiritual gifts by trying out different tasks within the church and finding out which ones energize us and get us excited. We can take a systematic inventory of our gifts with a helpful tool like the one we've included on page 136. We can also learn more about our spiritual gifts by getting feedback from members of the body who have seen us at work.

Take these few moments to talk to each other about spiritual gifts—your own and those that you see others using. To aid your discussion, we've included a list and a brief description of fourteen gifts on page 136 for you to copy for each member. (You'll find a more comprehensive list and inventory tool in the adult version of *Discover Your Gifts: And Learn How to Use Them* by Alvin J. Vander Griend.)

Talk about how each of these gifts can help your group achieve its calling and be a blessing to your church. Encourage each other by affirming the gifts you've seen in other people in this group. Your words of affirmation and encouragement may give your fellow members added confidence and resolve as they carry out their tasks or the courage to try something new.

Pray Together
3 minutes

Close your time by praising God together for the gifts the Spirit has given to Christ's body, the church. Specifically name the gifts represented in your group. Individually confess to God if you have failed to recognize and appreciate people whose gifts are not like yours and petition God for the Holy Spirit's guidance in using your gifts to build God's kingdom. Conclude your prayer time by singing "If You Believe and I Believe" (p. 119).

135

My Spiritual Gifts

Circle your two strongest working gifts. Share how you have identified and developed these two gifts over the years and how you feel they can benefit your working small group. If you're not sure which gifts you have, ask other members of your group to identify those they see in you.

- Administration: organizing, making plans, delegating
- Creative Ability: using music, art, writing, drama, dance
- Discernment: telling the difference between truth and error
- Encouragement: affirming, comforting
- Evangelism: talking about Jesus and leading others to believe
- Faith: believing and trusting God to act, inspiring others
- Giving: sharing money or possessions with others in need
- Hospitality: welcoming others, being kind and courteous
- Intercession: praying for others
- Leadership: taking charge, motivating others to follow
- Mercy: sympathetic, kind and helpful to those in need
- Prophecy: inspiring people to do God's will, taking a biblical stand on social justice issues
- Service: unselfishly helping others
- Teaching: modeling and explaining spiritual things to others, building good relationships

—Ruth Vander Zee, *Discover Your Gifts: And Learn How to Use Them* (Youth Version), CRC Publications, 1998.

Devotion Twenty-Seven

You Can Do It!

Build Community
2 minutes

Everyone—including each member of your working group—needs encouragement to keep on trying. Together, brainstorm all the phrases and expressions you can think of to cheer someone on. Start the list with "You can do it!"

Record the expressions and phrases on a chalkboard or overhead as people call them out. Circle the ones that are especially meaningful to your group right now.

Open God's Word
2 minutes

Words of encouragement lift people up. Paul ends his letter to the Thessalonians with this challenge:

God did not appoint us to suffer wrath but to receive salvation through our Lord Jesus Christ. He died for us so that, whether we are awake or asleep, we may live together with him.

Therefore encourage one another and build each other up, just as in fact you are doing.

Now we ask you, brothers, to respect those who work hard among you, who are over you in the Lord and who admonish you. Hold them in the highest regard in love because of their work. Live in peace with each other. And we urge you, brothers, warn those who are idle, encourage the timid, help the weak, be patient with everyone. Make sure that nobody pays back wrong for wrong, but always try to be kind to each other and to everyone else.

Be joyful always; pray continually; give thanks in all circumstances, for this is God's will for you in Christ Jesus.

—1 Thessalonians 5:9-18

Reflect on the Word
3 minutes

Charlie Brown, who lives his life expecting the worst, can always count on Lucy to make his expectations come true. Whether he's unburdening his heart to her at the doctor's booth or taking a chance on kicking the football, she's sure to say or do something that makes him feel bad. Keith Miller calls Lucy a "basement" person, someone who can pull another person down (Bruce Larson and Keith Miller, *The Passionate Person*).

The Lucys of this world leave us feeling depressed and unsure of ourselves. If we have an idea, they'll tell us it won't work. If we bake a cake, fix a broken toy, or plan a trip, they'll tell us about someone who did it better. Lucy and people like her manage to uncover the places in our secret psyche where we feel dumb and ugly and unlovable. They cross out our hopes and dreams with just one wicked slash of their tongues.

Contrast that to the encouraging letters of the apostle Paul. To Timothy he writes, "I thank God . . . as night and day I constantly remember you in my prayers. . . . I long to see you, so that I may be filled with joy" (2 Tim. 1:3-4). To the early churches Paul says: "We always thank God for all of you [and] continually remember before our God and Father your work produced by faith, your labor prompted by love, and your endurance inspired by hope in our Lord Jesus Christ" (1 Thess. 1:2-3). "We always thank God . . . when we pray for you, because we have heard of your faith in Christ Jesus and of the love you have for all the saints" (Col. 1:3). "I always thank God for you . . . because our testimony about Christ was confirmed in you" (1 Cor. 1:4, 6).

Using Miller's description, we would call Paul a "balcony" person, a cheerleader who applauded every baby step the new churches took in the right direction. True, he admonished their wrongdoings, but Paul also delighted in seeing these infants in Christ growing strong. The recipients of these letters felt blessed and strengthened, corrected and encouraged. Rather than dreading Paul's next appearance, they looked forward to another visit from him.

We can be balcony people for each other. In fact, it's God's desire that we encourage and build each other up by our attitudes, our words, and our deeds. It's God's will that we say to each other, "I thank God every day for you."

Live Out the Word
8 minutes

Choose one or more of these "encouragement exercises" as you respond to Paul's challenge:

Encouragers

Share stories of a time when someone encouraged you. Give specific details: What was the situation? Who encouraged you? What words and actions did they use? What was the result?

Prayer Warriors

Write each group member's name on a slip of paper and have everyone draw a name. During a brief refreshment break, talk to this person about his or her specific needs for encouragement. Commit to pray for and encourage this person until the next meeting.

God's Encouragement

The Bible is full of words of encouragement; in fact, Paul writes, "Everything that was written in the past was written to teach us, so that through endurance and the encouragement of the Scriptures we might have hope" (Rom. 15:4). Invite each person to read a favorite Scripture verse to the group and tell why this verse means a lot to them. As you share your stories, the sacred word of God will inspire hope in your group.

Try It!

In the Scripture passage from 1 Thessalonians 5, Paul lists a number of specific actions and attitudes that encourage others:

- Respect those who work hard among you.
- Live in peace with each other.

- Warn those who are idle.
- Encourage the timid.
- Help the weak.
- Be patient with everyone.
- Try to be kind.
- Be joyful always.
- Pray continually.
- Give thanks in all circumstances.

What other words, actions, and attitudes could you add to the list that especially apply to your working group? Put these principles into practice right now, either by words or deeds of encouragement. Provide notecards for group members to write words of encouragement to group members or to those in your church who work hard (custodians, organists, pastors, and so on) to make it possible for you to worship and work in this place. Invite elderly people with time on their hands or someone with a mental impairment to help with a specific task your group must do in the next week or so. Celebrate a small or major goal your group has achieved—plan a joyful party for your family members who have been patient through endless hours of meetings. Make a prayer list (both petitions and thanksgiving) for each member, and put your requests in the bulletin. Be creative and come up with your own ideas.

Pray Together

3 minutes

Sing this song as you reflect on the "full joy" that comes with loving others:

"This Is My Commandment"
This is my commandment
*   that you love one another,*
that your joy may be full.
This is my commandment
*   that you love one another,*
that your joy may be full.
That your joy may be full,
that your joy may be full.
This is my commandment
*   that you love one another,*
that your joy may be full.

—Anonymous

End your time together by silently praying for or audibly naming people to whom you want to spread God's love through your encouragement.

Devotion Twenty-Eight

I Accept and Honor You!

Build Community
4 minutes

Just for fun, take note of the variety within your group. Here are some ideas to try:

- Line up from shortest to tallest, rearrange in order from darkest hair to lightest hair or from oldest to youngest.
- Seat pepperoni pizza lovers on one side and everything-on-it pizza lovers on the other side of your meeting area.
- Have classical musicians hum a line from Beethoven and rock fans drum a beat.
- Line up shoes from the smallest to the largest—and then "walk a mile in someone else's moccasins."

Celebrate variety!

Open God's Word
2 minutes

Loving one another in the early Christian church wasn't always easy. Jewish Christians were conditioned by centuries of teachings that they were a chosen people. They had an "us" and "them" mentality, "us" being those God loved and "them" being those God rejected. But when Gentiles began responding to the gospel, the Jews were confronted with the need to obey Christ's message "Love one another." Paul addresses this issue.

Accept one another, then, just as Christ accepted you, in order to bring praise to God. For I tell you that Christ has become a servant of the Jews on behalf of God's truth, to confirm the promises made to the patriarchs so that the Gentiles may glorify God for his mercy, as it is written:

"Therefore I will praise you among the Gentiles; I will sing hymns to your name."

Again it says,

"Rejoice O Gentiles, with his people."

And again,

"Praise the Lord, all you Gentiles, and sing praises to him, all you peoples."

And again, Isaiah says,

"The Root of Jesse will spring up, one who will arise to rule over the nations; the Gentiles will hope in him."

May the God of hope fill you with all joy and peace as you trust in him, so that you may overflow with hope by the power of the Holy Spirit.

—Romans 15:7-13

Reflect on the Word
3 minutes

We only have to sit in a mall for a little while to realize that God made an amazing variety of people. As they stream past, we are struck by differences in skin and hair color, language, economic situation, gender, size, and age. Less visible, but equally important, are differences in political and religious beliefs, parenting styles, food preferences, emotional well-being—the list is endless. Variety is good. If everyone were the same, life wouldn't be nearly as interesting.

We only have to work within the church for a little while to realize that God made an endless variety of people with an equally endless variety of assumptions, convictions, worship styles, communication abilities, and gifts. Yet when it comes to church, we may not feel quite as comfortable with variety as we do in the mall. If people just thought the same, perhaps life in the church would be easier—there would be less conflict, less misunderstanding, less dispute over the "right way" to do things.

Satan delights in letting our differences divide us. But Paul has a solution. It's a variation on Jesus' command "Love one another as I have loved you." Paul says, *"Accept* one another just as Christ *accepted* you." Put that way, we have little choice. If Christ, the sinless one, wholeheartedly and unconditionally accepts us as sinners, can we do any less to our brothers and sisters, whom Christ also claims as his own?

The Greek word for acceptance, *proslambano,* is a word rich in meaning. It means not just a passive acquiescence, but an active welcome. Paul urges the Roman Jews to hold out their arms to the Gentiles, to draw in a newcomer, to smile and warmly enfold them in their fellowship.

We have differences. But we also have one very important common ground: we are children of our heavenly Father. Acceptance is one of the most important gifts we can give each other. It makes our community—this working group—a place where we belong, where we can relax and be ourselves. Here we can focus on what unites us: a love for Christ and a desire to work together to serve him.

Live Out the Word
8 minutes

No doubt by now, your group has identified differences within your group. Perhaps they've come to the surface; perhaps they're lying under the surface and are keeping you from accomplishing your work. Get beyond the obvious—shoe sizes, skin and hair color, personal preferences—and take a serious look at some of these differences. Discuss these questions together or in groups of two or three:

- In the early church, the biggest barrier to acceptance was the distinction between Jews and Gentiles. They differed in almost every way—political beliefs, religious background, behavior norms, family customs, and more. What are the biggest barriers that divide Christians in your church? Are these differences represented in your working group?
- How have these differences in your church and working group kept you from accomplishing your work? (You may want to refer back to your church's mission statement and your group's goals. Cite specific examples of how you haven't been able to accomplish a certain goal because of differences that divide.)
- What actions has the group taken to break down barriers and show acceptance? What more can your group do to accept others in your group and in church? (Describe two or three specific ways that relate to your goals and to the differences you've identified.)

Pray Together
3 minutes

Celebrate God's love with favorite songs your group enjoys, or sing or say the refrain from "Jesu, Jesu" (p. 97). Pray for God's Spirit to fill you with love.

List of Suggested Songs

In each devotion, we've suggested one or more songs for your group to sing (or you may prefer to read the words). Here's a list of the titles (numbers in parenthesis indicate the devotion number where the song is suggested). Numerous songs could be listed, and we encourage you to select others your group will enjoy.

"Amen, We Praise Your Name" *("Amen, Siakadumisa")* (6)
"Breathe on Me, Breath of God" (1)
"Father, We Adore You" (20)
"God, You Call Us to This Place" (16)
"Hear Our Prayer, O Lord" (20, 21)
"He Is Lord" (18)
"If You Believe and I Believe" (21, 26)
"Jesu, Jesu" (14, 19, 28)
"Lead Me, Guide Me" (2, 3, 9, 15)
"Lord, Be Glorified" (1, 9, 22)
"Lord, I Want to Be a Christian" (11)
"Lord, Listen to Your Children Praying" (2, 21, 24)
"Make Me a Channel of Your Peace" (7, 15)
"O Master, Let Me Walk with Thee" (2, 10, 15)
"Spirit of the Living God" (1, 4, 8, 15, 19)
"Take My Life That It May Be" (17)

"The Joy of the Lord Is My Strength" (5)
"The Servant Song" (13, 17, 25)
"This Is My Commandment" (19, 27)
"Those Who Wait upon the Lord" (12, 23)
"We Will Glorify" (6)
"What a Friend We Have in Jesus" (24)

Selected References

Adler, Ronald B. and George Rodman. *Understanding Human Communication.* 4th ed. Ft. Worth: Holt, Rinehart and Winston, 1991.

Barna, George. *The Power of Vision.* Ventura, Calif.: Regal Books, a division of Gospel Light, © 1992 by George Barna.

Chambers, Oswald. *Treasures from My Utmost for His Highest.* Ulrichsville, Ohio: Barbour Publishing, Inc. Published by special arrangement with and permission of Discovery House Publishers, © 1935 by Dodd, Mead, and Company, Inc. Copyright renewed 1963 by Oswald Chambers Publications Association, Ltd.

Clairmont, Patsy. *Sportin' a 'Tude: What Your Attitude Says When You're Not Looking.* Colorado Springs: Focus on the Family, 1996.

Corrigan, Thom. *Experiencing Community: A Pilgrimage Small Group Guide.* Colorado Springs: NavPress, © 1991 by Thom Corrigan.

Gorman, Julie. *Community That Is Christian: A Handbook on Small Groups.* Wheaton, Ill.: Victor Books/Scripture Press Publications, Inc., 1993.

Ford, Leighton. *Transforming Leadership.* Downers Grove, Ill.: InterVarsity Press, © 1991 by Leighton Ford.

Foster, Richard. *Celebration of Discipline.* New York: HarperCollins Publishers, © 1978, 1988 by Richard Foster.

Hart, Dirk J. *Charting a Course for Your Church.* Grand Rapids, Mich.: CRC Publications, 1997.

Hendricks, Howard. *Teaching to Change Lives*. Portland: Mult-
nomah, 1987.

Hestenes, Roberta. *Turning Committees into Communities*. Colorado
Springs: NavPress, © 1991 by Roberta Hestenes.

Hestenes, Roberta and Julie Gorman. *Building Christian Community Through Small Groups*. Unpublished syllabus. Pasadena,
Calif.: Fuller Theological Seminary, 1992.

Kamp, Eldean. "Growing a Community of Deacons," *Diaconal
Ministries in Eastern Canada Newsletter*. February 1999.

Larson, Bruce and Keith Miller. *The Passionate People*. Waco, Tex.:
Word Books, 1979.

Le Peau, Andrew T. *Paths of Leadership*. Downers Grove, Ill.: Inter-
Varsity Press, 1983.

Mattson, Ralph T. *Visions of Grandeur*. Chicago: Praxis Books/
Moody Press, 1994.

Maxwell, John. *Developing the Leader Within You*. Nashville:
Thomas Nelson, 1993.

Nywening, Willy. *So You've Been Asked To . . . Lead a Small Group*.
Grand Rapids, Mich.: CRC Publications, 1998.

Peck, Morgan Scott. *The Road Less Traveled*. New York: Simon and
Schuster, Inc., © 1978 by M. Scott Peck, M.D.

Poffenberger, Dan, Judy Stack Nelson, and Patrick Keifert. *Working
Together: Leading a Task-Oriented Small Group*. Minneapolis/St.
Paul: Church Innovations Publishing, Inc. 1995.

Schut, Jessie. *So You've Been Asked To . . . Recruit Volunteers*. Grand
Rapids, Mich.: CRC Publications, 1999.

Smith, Gordon T. *Listening to God in Times of Choice: The Art of
Discerning God's Will*. Downers Grove, Ill.: InterVarsity Press,
© 1997 by Gordon T. Smith.

Songs for LiFE. Grand Rapids, Mich.: CRC Publications, 1994.

Stam, Jeff. *So You've Been Asked To . . . Chair a Committee*. Grand
Rapids, Mich.: CRC Publications, 1999.

Vander Griend, Alvin J. *Discover Your Gifts and Learn How to Use
Them*. Grand Rapids, Mich.: CRC Publications, 1996.

Vander Griend, Alvin with Edith Bajema. *The Praying Church
Sourcebook*, 2nd ed. Grand Rapids, Mich.: CRC Publications, 1997.

Vander Zee, Ruth. *Discover Your Gifts and Learn How to Use Them*.
Youth Version. Grand Rapids, Mich.: CRC Publications, 1998.

Willow Creek Small Groups Leadership Handbook. South Barrington,
Ill.: Willow Creek Community Church, 1994.